THE
WELSH HIGHLAND RAILWAY

Volume 2

· A PAST and PRESENT COMPANION ·

WELSH HIGHLAND RAILWAY
(LIGHT RAILWAY) COMPANY.

RE-OPENING
OF
Dinas to South Snowdon
(Rhyd-ddu) Section (formerly North Wales Narrow
Gauge Railway),
On 31st JULY, 1922.
10 Miles of Beautiful Scenery.
Streams, Waterfalls, Lakes & Mountains.
OBSERVATION CARS PROVIDED.

Excursion Tickets are issued daily to South Snowdon
Station from Great Western Rly. Stations Via
Afonwen & Dinas Jct. as follows,-

From		Times of Starting. a.m.	3rd Class Return Fare.
PORTMADOC	... ..	10 25	5s. 8d.
CRICCIETH	... ..	10 34	5s. 1d.
PWLLHELI	... ..	10 25	5s. 2d.
Arrive SOUTH SNOWDON	...	1 0 p.m.	

Passengers return as under`:—

SOUTH SNOWDON STATION dept.	3 55 p.m. (Sats. exept.)	6 40 p.m.	
PWLLHELI Arrive	...	6 35 p.m.	8 55 p.m.
CRICCIETH do.	...	6 32 p.m.	8 48 p.m.
PORTMADOC do.	...	6 50 p.m.	9 0 p.m.

The shortest and best ascent of SNOWDON is made from SOUTH SNOWDON STATION.
The distance is about 3 miles, and the path leads directly from the Station.

General Manager's Office,
    Portmadoc, Aug. 1922.

S E. TYRWHITT,
General Manager.

No. 3.   Jones & Co., Printers, Portmadoc.

A Welsh Highland Heritage Copy

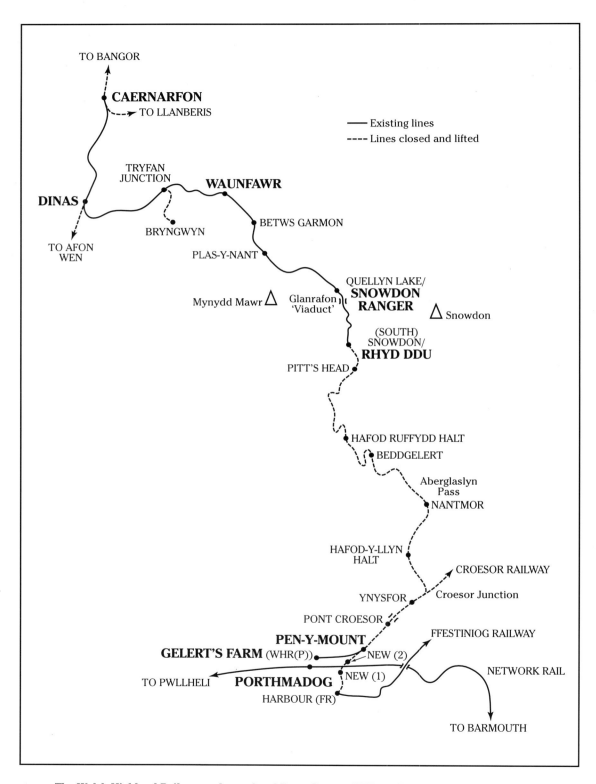

The Welsh Highland Railway and associated lines. Current WHR stations are shown in large type.

THE
WELSH HIGHLAND RAILWAY

Volume 2

• A PAST and PRESENT COMPANION •

Halfway to Paradise

John Stretton

Welsh Highland Railway.
TRAIN STAFF TICKET.
TRAIN No. (UP)
To the ENGINE DRIVER or BRAKESMAN
You are authorised, after seeing the Train Staff
coloured **Green** for the Section, to proceed from
South Snowdon to Beddgelert
and the Train Staff will follow
Signature of person in charge ....
Date.......................................19 (over.)

• RAILWAY HERITAGE •
from
The NOSTALGIA Collection

First published in 2004

British Library Cataloguing in Publication Data

A catalogue record for this book is available from the British Library.

ISBN 1 85895 233 6

Past & Present Publishing Ltd
The Trundle
Ringstead Road
Great Addington
Kettering
Northants NN14 4BW

Tel/Fax: 01536 330588
email: sales@nostalgiacollection.com
Website: www.nostalgiacollection.com

Printed and bound in Great Britain

Past and
Present

A Past & Present book
from
The NOSTALGIA *Collection*

ACKNOWLEDGEMENTS

As with all of my previous books, there are many people 'in the background' who play a vital part in the completion of the whole, while the author – as 'front man' – takes the glory. In this particular volume, as well as the undoubted heroes – far-sighted and gifted photographers who pointed their cameras and, therefore, have allowed us to savour their work – there is one person who deserves the greater credit. Without doubt, John Keylock has been the major rock on which this volume has been built. Throughout, his humanity, courtesy, patience and never-ceasing willingness to both have his collection rifled and then to answer innumerable questions from your author, both before and after his proof-reading of the manuscript, have been exemplary and a source of encouragement.

Special thanks must also go to the two Davids – Kent and Allan – who, each in their turn, have been both supportive and helpful. Their inputs have added real flavouring to the recipe. Others who have helped, either through their own work or their collections, are credited in the ensuing pages, but are also to be thanked. The illustrations, with a credit of MJS, are mine. Credit and thanks must go to my wife Judi, who tolerated long periods of isolation as I either sat huddled gnome-like in front of the computer or peered at innumerable photographs; without her forbearance, I could not have achieved the task within the deadline! Finally, to Peter Townsend at Silver Link for encouragement and putting up with countless phone calls; to David and Anna in the Silver Link office for their unflinching patience and courtesy; and to Will Adams and Mick Sanders for their usual skilful and speedy editing and design. Thank you all!

CONTENTS

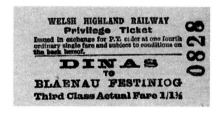

I make no apologies for reprising this picture. Seen in Volume 1 as a mere half-page, to represent the area around Salem, it deserves a much greater 'acreage', being both a delightful view of a rarely photographed location from an even rarer vantage point and a wonderful picture to boot. With the magnificent 'Elephant Mountain', aka Mynydd Mawr, peering over the bluff in the right distance, a single-Fairlie – quite possibly *Moel Tryfan* – heads south with a short mixed train in the late 1890s towards Plas-y-nant past a dry-stone-walled sheepfold. Having obviously recently stoked up the boiler, the fireman looks back at the photographer. Happily, since the re-opening to Rhyd Ddu, passengers can again travel this route and savour the dramatic scenery. *National Library of Wales, MJS collection*

INTRODUCTION

The previous volume – sub-titled 'A Phoenix Rising' – was originally published in 1999, when the emerging Welsh Highland Railway – that Phoenix – ran for just under 4 miles, from Caernarfon to Dinas. As pointed out in that book, not only was this route the first part of the new WHR, but also that it was constructed on the ex-BR standard-gauge trackbed that had, in happier times, been part of the Bangor-Afon Wen line. The newest section, however, does run on genuine WHR alignment and is truly recreating a past experience. The intervening four years since Volume 1 have seen massive and impressive strides in the reconstruction of the Welsh Highland, and the aim of this second volume is to both celebrate the progress to date and to look back at this march and on to the next phase.

As with Volume 1 – and others of my 'Past & Present' books – this latest is in essence a comparative exposition of what was and what now is, but juxtaposed with complementary and illuminating views. While the whole route from Caernarfon to Porthmadog is covered within these pages, as before, I have purposely avoided, wherever possible, using previously published photographs. Inevitably, however, with a subject as ancient and 'narrow' as a railway that ceased to operate 66 years ago – and despite every effort to winkle out some previously unseen views – there are one or two that the reader may well have seen before. I crave your indulgence and trust that you will enjoy those that are seeing the light of day for the first time.

I have been blessed by the co-operation of many people for this project, but for their unstinting willingness and enthusiasm, the authors of the three text chapters deserve my gratitude. John Keylock also merits especial mention here for his bloodhound-like detective work. Sherlock Holmes would have been proud! I have derived much pleasure in preparing this book, but the knowledge that they were beavering away in the background with their contributions was an added bonus. I have also enjoyed visiting and seeing the railway as it developed, and here Roland Doyle deserves commendation and my gratitude for allowing me access to the trackbed to photographically record ongoing events. The last four years have

Railway servants past... Highlighted as a portion of a wider view, which also includes the engine's crew, the train's guard, Dafydd Lloyd Hughes, peers out from under his flat cap as his portrait is captured, complete with starched white collar, overcoat, money pouch and ticket punching machine strapped across his chest. From the expression on his face, he could well be missing several teeth! In the background of this 1934 view, one of the railway's workers rounds the rear coach, while a potential passenger examines the inner workings of *Russell*'s cab, moments before the train leaves for Portmadoc. *A. W. Croughton, John Keylock collection*

seen many milestones and the transformation of many places from near wilderness to what is now most certainly a world-class railway.

The onwards construction of what is now a 13-mile adventure, to the western flanks of mighty Snowdon, has been a two-part production, with a temporary 'curtain down and intermission' at Waunfawr. On a personal note, as well as riding the trains and savouring both ride and magnificent views, I particularly enjoyed witnessing the emergence of the 'new' Tryfan Junction and the WHR returning to Waunfawr on 15 September 2000. The latter was made especially poignant for the Stretton household, as wife Judi and daughter Tammy were chosen to hold the two ends of the banner, as the massive Garratt bore down on them at the head of the inaugural train. The look on Judi's face – a mixture of fear, delight and exhilaration – as the locomotive 'broke the tape' will stay with me for ever! It wasn't until she saw a photograph in the local press that she realised that special guest Dafydd Wigley was waving from No 143's cab – she was just relieved that she was still alive!

The final phase to date, onwards to Rhyd Ddu, has vouchsafed many lasting memories for me, but as well as again sampling parts of the route on foot prior to opening, two particular events stand out. The bridging of the yawning gap over the river at Betws Garmon on 5 June 2003 was memorable, watching the huge crane gently lowering the new bridge into place and realising that a major piece of the jigsaw had just been put into the picture; and, only marginally less thrilling, just three days earlier witnessing the first (works) train run out of Rhyd Ddu station and round the curve on to the Fridd Isaf horseshoe. Sadly, I missed both Prince Charles's visit at the end of July and the opening on 18 August, but I was back for the Super Power Weekend on 14 September, and it was magical to see the railway open, the transformation in just three months and the hundreds of happy, smiling faces thoroughly enjoying themselves, the new line and the late-summer sunshine.

Thus far, so good. Ahead is the next 12 or so miles to Porthmadog. Walking parts of the route for this book has been an adventure in itself, as nature has staged a very deliberate comeback in

places. Bog, tree growth and brambles were just some of the delights sampled! Seeing the railway 'asleep' in this way brings home just how much will need to be done, and reinforces the major achievements to date. The Welsh Highland Railway is now roughly the same length as its near neighbour the Ffestiniog Railway; visitor numbers and takings (both extremely vital to the venture's success) were well above budget by the end of 2003; and there is that prospect of the next leg, through to Porthmadog. It already is exciting on the ground and the future is equally so. Hopefully, by the end of this decade, we will see trains once again running across Britannia Bridge in Porthmadog, and joining up with the FR at Harbour station. In the meantime, enjoy the views herein and out on the line and remember – we are only halfway to paradise!

...railway servants present! Sixty-five years later, in the summer of 1999, enthusiasts and WHR supporters Cedric Lodge (left), Derek Lyster (centre), with his wife demurely hiding in the background, and John Keylock (right) consult photograph and map on part of the old trackbed. The caption on the rear of the photograph proclaims, 'Where the hell are we!' Is it just your author's imagination, or is there a certain similarity in one of their number to the guard of the 1934 train on the previous page...? *David Allan/WHR Heritage collection*

THE CONTINUING STORY
by Dave Kent
Chairman, Welsh Highland Railway Society

In the first volume of this Companion – 'A Phoenix Rising' – the reader was given the history of our line, and how with considerable tenacity the line held on for many years before it finally collapsed just before the Second World War. As I said in that edition, everyone and everything has its moment of fame, and as I write this I consider that one of those moments has just occurred – the Prince of Wales has just visited the line from Waunfawr to Rhyd Ddu, on 30 July 2003, prior to its official public opening. History is what happens tomorrow, is happening today and has happened since we put the last book together!

We left that volume – published in 1999 – having arrived at Dinas, along the standard-gauge trackbed of the old Afon Wen line. It was here that the original junction with the North Wales Narrow Gauge Railway line led us on to true Welsh Highland territory. Before any work could be done to create the new section, all the planning requirements had to be sought and granted, so we could comply with the Transport & Works Order (Act of Parliament) allowing us the right to reconstruct the line from Dinas to Porthmadog. Once these hurdles had been overcome, construction started, but not in Dinas yard: rather, two or three points along the old formation were attacked first. Unlike motorway construction, our trackbed can be sometimes only 6 or 7 feet wide, and it is usual for any and all construction vehicles to access structures like bridges and culverts, drains, etc, along the line of the trackbed, sometimes for as much as a mile or more. In fact, anything you need to work on or provide before you actually lay the track and ballast has to be carried up the bed this way.

As the area is well known for its 'freshly washed' appearance, drains are the most important item below ground. We knew it was going to be tough, but the upper Gwyrfai valley as it approaches Waunfawr proved to be very difficult indeed, as in one place springs on the hillside had caused a large landslip. Civil engineering on this part of the line was hard going at times because of the enormous amounts of water and mud we had to contend with. People came to help from the four corners of the UK – as well as the world – to help. Their achievements were many and their help inspirational as they carried out much of the volunteer work. Underpinning all these visitors were the fortnightly efforts of the North Wales Track Gang. Almost entirely made up of local people, they turned out every other weekend to do everything from digging out blocked drains and rebuilding bridges to laying the track. These stalwarts have become the true professional tracklayers of the Welsh Highland, and put down more than two-thirds of the 4 miles between Dinas and Waunfawr. On Monday 7 August 2000 the Railway Inspectorate allowed the first passenger-carrying train to travel up the original course of the North Wales Narrow Gauge Railway and thus increase our line to 7 miles of the new Welsh Highland Railway. The line opening was by the popular local Member of Parliament Dafydd Wigley, who in conjunction with the representatives of the Millennium Commission, offered congratulations on the new section and its considerable achievement. In true railway style, everyone retired to the pub (adjacent to the platform) and enjoyed a very good buffet to round off the proceedings. Passengers came in flocks to see the new section of the line and a good summer season ended with lots of interest in what we were doing.

But when you start a project like this, you can't stop the natural momentum that tends to build up, and so it was that the company building the line (Welsh Highland Light Railway Limited) almost immediately began work on the next and third phase of this enormous project. It is probably worth reminding our readers, who may not be familiar with the railway, that the train has so far travelled 7 miles and in that distance has climbed almost 400 feet above sea level. This is true narrow-gauge-railway country. This third phase will take us a further 6 miles up into the mountains, still climbing all the way to a height of approximately 630 feet above sea level. As we progress along this next part of the track, the line will cross the Gwyrfai River another three times, together with a tributary, on the biggest engineering structure along the line, known as Glanrafon 'Viaduct'. The first bridge to cross the river, at Betws Garmon, was in fact one of the last to be sorted out. In poor condition, this structure dated from around 1876/7 so was removed to inspect the abutments; it was found that they had no real footings, and also restricted the river flow. The decision was made to renew the abutments, but further back on the riverbank, and then to construct a new span and deck. The cost of creating a new bow-type bridge spiralled, and eventually a redundant standard-gauge bridge was found, which with a little modification fitted perfectly. The support Society – Welsh Highland Railway Society – sponsored this work, from the purchase of the bridge, the alteration work, cleaning and welding, to the transport from Rotherham and the crane hire to put it in place. A bargain when you get teamwork at £15,000 for the whole job!

Both the second and third river crossings presented their own little difficulties, but they retained the original side spans, with new main beams. With rebuilt abutments and flood relief arches these river crossings were declared as good as new. The fourth bridge – the 'viaduct' – is something special, as it is some 100 feet long, spanning a gorge 60 feet below, and although largely hidden by tree growth, when the leaves have fallen it will provide impressive views of the swollen stream and waterfall way below. Approached at almost right angles from either way, the structure had to have some very specialist work done on it.

Giving just a glimpse of the task facing the reconstruction team, especially during a particularly wet winter period, a fully loaded dumper truck leaves the access slip road, down the gradient to the left, immediately to the north of Waunfawr station site on 5 February 2000. Making its way on to the old trackbed, it is taking vital supplies of stone to bolster a slipping embankment further towards Dinas. What will become the new railway's last few yards to the station, in the foreground, evidences the ruling weather conditions at this time. *MJS*

Strengthening of the beams was done, as we are able to get two Garratts on to the bridge and, at 125 tons for the pair, we have to make sure that after 120 years it is still capable of carrying a train safely! The final test took place only a week before passenger carrying took place (18 August 2003), and with both engines on the bridge it deflected by only 10mm. A success story for all those who helped to put it right.

The final mile and a half to the station at Rhyd Ddu finds the line twisting and turning on a rock shelf, from where some of the best views of Snowdon and Cwellyn Lake can be had. Rebuilding this part of the line has been a considerable challenge, as parts of the shelf on which the line runs are no more that 8 or 9 feet wide. Access for wheeled vehicles and diggers along this stretch of railway sometimes involved travelling half a mile or more, giving rise to some serious forward planning to get the job done. The Company, along with subcontractors, gained access to this part of the line and started the initial work in early 2001, as soon as possible after the lifting of the foot and mouth restrictions. While doing the early digging work they found out how little preparation the original company had made for drains, on this the wettest part of the line. There were, in places, none at all! This has now been seen to properly and a dry trackbed will be the result in future years. The local track gang were then given the opportunity to get on with the job of laying rail in the early part of the following year. The volunteer North Wales Track Gang has achieved and completed about 90% of all the track on this section of line, covering a distance of almost 5½ miles in all.

As I write this, trains are passing my office about every hour and a quarter; we have been open to the public for just 10 days. Each of these trains is almost full to capacity, with people eager to see the new length of line. The comments are many, but almost all say how spectacular this railway really is. We have to thank the planners and engineers of the original North Wales Narrow Gauge Railways, way back in the mid-Victorian times of 1870, for their foresight and determination in seeing the line through. It really seems to be a case of the line being way ahead of its time.

One of the things we haven't mentioned is how we have been able to pay for the work so far. The Government decided a good few years ago to celebrate the turn of the Millennium by sponsoring, with Lottery money, a number of schemes that would stand the test of time. The Welsh Highland, through its parent company the Ffestiniog Railway, applied for and won backing to the tune of 43% of the total cost, based on 1995 estimates. This, together with grants from the Welsh Assembly and European Aid bodies, the support of the Welsh Highland Railway Society and reciprocal efforts of volunteers, added up to sufficient backing to build the line this

It was a race against time and the elements to have the railway opened to the public close to the proclaimed deadline. Due to unforeseen conditions, this deadline was missed, but having seen the aftermath of the appalling weather, together with the Herculean task facing the workers, it was no small feat that the celebrations could be enjoyed just a little over seven months from the date of the view on the opposite page. On 15 September 2000, the then leader of Plaid Cymru, Dafydd Wigley – having ridden into the station on the footplate of Garratt No 143, breaking the banner to signal the start of events – gives his celebratory oration to the assembled throng at Waunfawr station, formally declaring this next stage of the railway open. Behind him stand a representative of the Millennium Commission and the Lord Mayor of Caernarfon, with Mike Hart, representing the Ffestiniog Railway, to the right. *MJS*

far. Fund-raising is always difficult, especially for sponsors who cannot see the project first, and when it's a line into and through a National Park, real commitment and determination are major ingredients in what is needed to get the complete railway line built. The Company, the Society and all of our volunteers hope you will enjoy their recent efforts in creating this further extension of our line, and look forward to seeing you on it one day very soon.

Like all good stories, the tale of the Welsh Highland goes on and the completion of the line from Rhyd Ddu through the forests to Beddgelert and on to Porthmadog has yet to be told. Before we can start this section of line, we have first to obtain the relevant planning permissions and, at the same time, arrange for enough future funding so the job can be completed in a reasonable time. If you have enjoyed the trip so far, and are excited by what you have read, why not think of helping complete the story? Come along and join in the fun and hard work; you can be part of making our history in the future. This project is one of the most outstanding of its type anywhere in Western Europe, if not the world. Let us all make tomorrow's history together.

A taster of some of the problems. As Dave Kent says, the old WHR was not over-endowed with proper drainage, leading to the new railway – not least with current Health & Safety regulations – having to provide much more than would appear necessary on the surface. In addition, due to the sheer size of the ex-South African Garratts, the original loading gauge was insufficient under road overbridges, resulting in around 3 feet extra depth having to be provided for clearance. Both factors are seen compounding the successful reconstruction at Waunfawr on 5 February 2000. The metal cross-girder is at the previous trackbed level and the wooden box shields work on a brand new drain, to relieve/prevent flooding problems from the nearby River Gwyrfai. The station site is through the bridge.

By 14 July the place has been transformed. Happily now in much drier conditions, the alignment is complete, track laid and the drain discreetly covered – seen just to the right of the rails. Now truly looking part of the scene, the lowering of the trackbed would probably go unnoticed to a majority of onlookers. Ballast, tamping and testing are now all that is required – a credit to all involved. *Both MJS*

River bridges have also been a problem in the reconstruction; not least that immediately south of Betws Garmon station. The former bow bridge and its river abutments proved insufficient for the task ahead and replacements had to be sourced and installed. While a re-creation of the original bridge would have been ideal, this proved to be impossible – not least financially. After much searching, a redundant ex-BR bridge was discovered at Beighton, near Sheffield. Even this, however, was not without problems, as it had originally been a skew bridge, whereas Betws Garmon needed a straight one! Thankfully, there was sufficient metal left after cutting it to shape to span the river – just! WHR Society funding paid for the bridge and transfer to the site, then, after much volunteer preparation and painting, it was carefully lowered into place on 4 June 2003. Ropes, chains and the human eye guided it, and here it is almost in place. To everyone's relief it fitted first time! *MJS*

The bow bridge was characteristic of the NWNGR/WHR, and another example crossed the River Gwyrfai at Plas-y-nant. Happily, this proved to be still man enough for the job – impressive, considering its age, the fact that it has lain derelict for nigh on 70 years, and that the Garratts are far heavier than anything seen during the lifetime of the original railway. On 1 June 2003 it bears rails once more, although there is still a deal of work to be completed before passenger trains will once again pass over it, which occurred a little over two months after this view, in mid-August. Note the sharp bend on to the bridge, from the north, mirroring the curve of the river and the need to build up the trackbed off the bridge. *MJS*

THE ROUTE PAST AND PRESENT:
DINAS TO WAUNFAWR

Left Like all good public attractions, the new WHR is constantly evolving, providing the visitor with fresh experiences and visual delights. While superficially there is little difference between the view of Garratt No 138 at Caernarfon in October 1997 on page 83 of Volume 1 and that here, the locomotive has since received a new coat. Now in a (somewhat controversial) lighter shade of green and fully lined out, since 1 March 2002 it has borne the name *Millennium*, in acknowledgment of the huge financial involvement of the Millennium Commission in the rebuilding of the railway. On 14 September 2003 it stands at the northern terminus in Caernarfon, suitably adorned with a celebratory headboard, with the Castle glimpsed in the background, waiting to depart with a train bound for Rhyd Ddu as part of the Super Power Weekend celebrations. *MJS*

Below left As Volume 1 explained, the stretch of the new line from Caernarfon to Dinas makes use of the ex-BR standard-gauge route. Originally two parallel, unconnected lines on the southern exit from Caernarfon, the parting of the ways came immediately after the St Helen's Road bridge, on the outskirts of the town. The left-hand line ran to Llanberis and the other continued in a southerly direction, eventually to join the Cambrian Coast line at Afon Wen. The sharp divergence of the two routes is graphically shown in this ground-level view from the early 1960s. While the road passing under the railway in the foreground is still present, albeit disused, the view ahead has been dramatically altered by road works, now bringing the St Helen's Road access to the new WHR and the quayside area over the railway. The bridge carrying the main road to Porthmadog, seen just beyond the left-hand track, is still extant. Note the check rails on the Afon Wen route, the 40mph and 30mph signs and the distant signal beyond. *Norman Kneale*

Above Dinas, the initial terminus of the new railway, is some 3 miles from Caernarfon, set, even to this day, in largely rural surroundings. Just how isolated was this junction between the WHR and LNWR in former days can be judged from this superb aerial view of the location taken during the last war, in 1942, by railway enthusiast and WHR supporter F/Lt Arthur Rimmer. Caernarfon is to the left and Afon Wen to the right. A standard-gauge freight train stands temporarily at rest in the station. From here, the WHR route negotiated a form of horseshoe, leaving the picture in the lower right-hand third only to reappear in the upper right-hand third, as what appears to be a road in this view. It then threaded its way through the patchwork of fields on its way to Tryfan Junction, Waunfawr and the south. Though the BR line was still open, the WHR was closed, with most of its tracks removed. The sparse distribution of buildings is noticeable, compared to the situation on the ground 60 years later. *Arthur Rimmer, WHR collection*

Above Back on terra firma, this is the view of Dinas station on arrival from Caernarfon, snapped from the rear coach of a northbound DMU on 23 August 1963. In the centre stands the substantial stone transhipment shed, with the erstwhile refreshment room to the right, on the station platform. The site of the old slate wharf is to the left, now in alternative employment. Note how neat and tidy are the trackbed and surrounding area, on this backwater of British Railways in its last days of operation, and how a 'green barrier' now separates these tracks from the old WHR site. A lone inhabitant of the yard watches the train leave for Caernarfon. *Sidney Leleux*

Below Around the same period as above, a four-car DMU set, with M79682 leading, pauses at Dinas in atrocious weather on an Afon Wen-Llandudno Junction service. The driver attends to some matter in the cab during the pause, while the signalman, safely tucked away in his box, watches the whole show. Note the driver's opposing windscreen wipers and the provision of four cars for this relatively little-used branch-line service – compare this to the sad sight of just two cars on a long, cross-country journey on today's Network Rail. Notice how the platform is suffering neglect, compared to the track seen above. *Norman Simmons, Hugh Davies collection*

Swinging round 180 degrees from the last view, a BR Standard Class 4 4-6-0 arrives at Dinas with steam to spare on a 'North Wales Radio Land Cruise'. Presumably, with at least five coaches behind it, these rail tours were popular with tourists and the travelling public, but just how much they will see and/or enjoy of the surrounding countryside in these 'monsoon' conditions is open to question! One of the Standard's crew seems keen to have his portrait taken, despite the rain. The semaphore in the distance protects the single line ahead.

Forty years later, on 1 June 2003, gone are the standard-gauge tracks and platforms and the old WHR wooden refreshment rooms, replaced by new equivalents of the former and the appearance of ex-County Council buildings in the background. A mixture of freight stock, including ex-South African ballast wagons, occupies the newly created sidings, while the station is adorned with nameboard and period-style lamp standards and, in the distance, now enjoys the provision of a two-road carriage shed. The fact that the whole scene looks 'natural' is yet more credit to all involved in both the initial planning and the eventual construction. *Norman Simmons, Hugh Davies collection/MJS*

Standing at the southern end of the station, the route is still open – the signalman is in his box and his door is open, presumably to enjoy the summer air. The semaphore signal at the far end of the platform is raised to herald the imminent approach of the next service from Afon Wen – but the general air is one of gradual run-down. Grass is taking a hold of the platform surfaces and the verdant growth on both sides of the station is being left to do as it will. Note the WHR station building and wooden refreshment rooms on the far platform still in situ.

After years of abandonment, then occupation by the County Council, by 1 June 2003 the site has been transformed by the new WHR and now has a very 'lived-in' feel. The platforms may be lower than their forebears and the tracks of narrower gauge, and much else may be of new construction, but the past is still present in the guise of the ex-NWNGR station building and goods shed. Preserving the heritage of the old railway, these two buildings have been tastefully and sympathetically converted to modern use and serve as a wonderful counterpoint, with their distinctive yellow facing bricks, to the wholly new creations elsewhere on site. In the centre of the view, immediately beyond the white fencing, stands ex-SAR NGG15 No 140. Awaiting eventual restoration, this will give a further variety to the more usual diet of Garratts. *Lens of Sutton, MJS collection/MJS*

Ascending by means of the fenced slope on the right to the road bridge seen in the background of the pictures on page 16, this is the more elevated view of Dinas station on a summer evening around 1880. Station staff – and even a Victorian lady – stand patiently while their photograph is taken. To the left, an LNWR train – hauled by a Webb 2-4-2T – pauses before resuming the journey to Afon Wen, while to the right the NWNGR's *Beddgelert* also stands ready to head south. Note, once again, the open fields surrounding the station site at this time, the absence of a station nameboard and the very sparse passenger facilities. The goods shed and station building are again prominent, but note how the latter lacks the windows that were later to grace this south-facing wall.

Around 112 years have passed, and history is made on 12 October 1997 as the very first steam-hauled fare-paying passenger train runs on the new railway – the 1000 from Caernarfon. The four-coach train draws to a halt behind Garratt No 138 – in original green livery – heralding an exciting and brighter future for this part of North Wales and the potential regeneration of the tourist trade in the area. On this day, 24 hours before the formal opening, notice the complete absence of photographers – somewhat amazing, considering the importance of the event! *Dunn collection/MJS*

In the later years of operation, services over the old WHR consisted of around three or four coaches, but in earlier times there was both a much greater provision and variety for the intending traveller. In 1895 a single-Fairlie stands by the goods shed in Dinas yard, having arrived from Rhyd Ddu with a morning service of seven coaches. As so often in those far-off days, notice how the station staff stand for their portraits to be taken by the man under the black cloth!

In the second view, 108 years later, the goods shed is still proudly standing, defying all comers and now once again part of an active scene. On 1 June 2003 some of the by-products of railway reconstruction stand in Dinas yard, awaiting their turn to add to the developing and burgeoning railway. *Peter Treloar collection/MJS*

Despite this wonderfully attractive and evocative portrait of *Russell*, the end is nigh. In 1936, the last year of passenger operation, a mixed train of three passenger coaches and attached freight wagons waits to leave Dinas bound for Beddgelert, no doubt hoping to have attracted some travellers from the LMS Third Class coaches seen to the left on the 'main line'. The sunshine beautifully picks out *Russell*'s light green and black livery, 'W.H.R.' legend on the tank side and highly polished nameplate, maker's plate and dome. Note the capacious sand barrel on the front buffer beam and the remnants of the multi-coloured coaches, so painted by the Festiniog Railway in an attempt to drum up tourist support in the mid-1930s. Note also the wonderful acetylene headlamp! *P. S. Kendrick, Millbrook House Ltd Collection*

21

On leaving the station area, the NWNGR/WHR headed south from Dinas under a road bridge. This is the view from underneath that bridge, around 1909. The sloping wall to the left marks the passenger entrance to the station from the bridge, while the goods shed stands ready for business on the right, and the main station buildings are en bloc in the centre. Note the tall signal – built to this height to allow sighting by approaching southbound LNWR trains. The standard-gauge platforms can just be discerned to the left of this signal.

In 2003 that retaining wall is still there, but access is no longer available to the area by that route, not least due to the growth of trees upon it. Modern travellers arrive by way of the approach road on the right, past the end of the substantial hedge, with access to the platforms beyond the car and railings seen here. The main station building still stands, in the centre, with the goods shed, now with vibrant red doors, glimpsed beyond the car. *G. M. Perkins, WHR collection/MJS*

Above Turning through 180 degrees from the previous page, this is the view of the line as it departs from Dinas terminus. In this view from 31 August 1926, the running line curves away to the left, to head for the open country, past cows grazing on what is now part of the new railway's yard, while the engine shed is straight ahead, with Baldwin No 590 lurking behind the half-closed door. To the right, the signal box was erected to control entrance to this shed, and to the carriage shed, out of the picture behind the photographer to the left, and the running line, but had been long out of use by this date. Coach 24, ex-NWNGR No 12, one of two 'Ashburys' purchased in 1894, stands outside the carriage shed. Subsequently renumbered 23 by the FR in 1936, this coach happily still survives, restored to WHR condition in green livery. *H. C. Casserley*

Below After the cessation of services, the then current locomotives were abandoned. Inside the shed in 1939 are Baldwin No 590 and *Russell*, but they certainly will not be receiving much in the way of protection from the elements, judging by the open nature of the roof and wooden slats from it resting on *Russell*'s superstructure! To the left, all manner of railway detritus cascades over the remaining area of the shed – all left for fate to take its course! *Photomatic, John Keylock collection*

The end of the road. In operational times the running line left the Dinas yard by passing underneath the A487, the main Caernarfon-Portmadoc road. After termination of services, this passage was blocked by infill, undergrowth and, latterly, a water services pipeline. Incredibly, that pipe and road are just beyond the newly restored ex-South African Funky diesel, at the extremity of the line on 5 June 1999.

Equally incredibly, this is the same view a mere 13 months later, on 14 July 2000, after clearance of the 'muck and rubbish' in the cutting, the refurbishment of the road retaining wall and movement of the water pipe, the establishment of retaining walls for the railway and the laying of track. The newly laid track awaits a supply of ballast and other minor cosmetic work, before being ready for the trains. *Both MJS*

The next bridge encountered by the restorers, as they progressed towards Tryfan Junction, was that at Cae Moel, which presented the railway's engineers with a unique problem. As can be judged from the first view, in late 1999, the bridge was in fact a triple, with road over railway over stream! While initial considerations led to ideas of retaining this arrangement, it was precluded by the need to lower the trackbed to accommodate the greater height of the Garratts. After much thought and advice, the decision was taken to divert the course of the stream. This demanded a completely fresh line and a temporary road bridge over the selected area, during the construction works.

The sheer scale of 'merely diverting a stream' can be judged by the second view on 26 April 2000, with the original railway bridge to the right and major earthworks for the new WHR, including provision of a suitably sized pipe to carry the watercourse. *Both David Allan*

Opposite page Midway between Cae Moel and Tryfan Junction is an example of some of the remedial and/or extra provision work that was necessary for the new railway to accommodate the requirements of farm neighbours. At Bodaden, what became 'UB10' on the new alignment is seen on 19 January 2000, during a lunch break for some of the local gang, also showing the aftermath of recent heavy rainfall.

Just four months later, on 26 April, the farmer has a brand new access road, complete with purpose-laid hard surface and appropriate drainage and with a greater clearance than previously, while the railway has both restored the trackbed and retained the essential NWNGR/WHR character and stone/ brickwork, including building up the bridge parapet.
Both David Allan, WHR Heritage collection

This page This is the state of the old trackbed *after* some clearance! Seen on 29 August 1999, on the approaches to Tryfan Junction, trees have been felled and the path of the trackbed cleared to (just about) identify the direction of the route.

In the second view, dated 8 March 2000 and looking in the opposite direction, with the narrow approach road on the right, a JCB belonging to contractors D. A. Jones Bros assists with both the levelling of the trackbed and preparation of a new retaining wall on the right. The station building is in the distance, largely hidden from view by a dumper truck.

Three years later the railway is open. On 2 June 2003 the line is very definitely beginning to look like an established ingredient of the rural scene. The station building can now just be glimpsed under the distant arboreal canopy.
MJS/David Allan, WHR Heritage collection/MJS

Reversing position, the bridge vantage point of the last two images is now seen in the distance, with groundworks being undertaken on the trackbed and retaining wall on 16 February 2000. Again, with the preparation for the new retaining wall in the foreground, some idea of the scale of works necessary for the re-opening of the railway – and the need for the multi-million pound grant from the Millennium Commission – is readily apparent.

Again seen on 2 June 2003, nature has come to man's rescue, softening and/or hiding the harsh scars of JCB and dumper truck. Once more, the appearance is of a line that has run here for many a year, not for just three!
David Allan, WHR Heritage collection/MJS

A view of the old WHR on 15 May 1923. The railway still has a fortnight to wait before opening through to Portmadoc as *Moel Tryfan* pauses at Tryfan Junction station with the 9.45am train from Dinas to South Snowdon (Rhyd Ddu). The engine crew discuss some detail with an elderly gentleman, while the guard and other travellers look on, as the locomotive shrouds the signal box in excess steam. Trains on the 'main line' never used the track adjacent to the station building, out of sight to the left.

Sadly, the hopes, aspirations and halcyon days of the mid-1920s were not to last, with the result that the railway ceased passenger operations in 1936. Thereafter the WHR lapsed into a deep slumber, woken only briefly in the early 1940s by reclamation of rails, etc, for scrap. In this view from 1941, the station building is intact, but the grass has made strides to reclaim the line of the track as flat wagons await another load of rail.

Once more, the transformation is dramatic. Rails are present and ready for traffic on 2 June 2003 and the station building is fenced off, in preparation for eventual restoration. Certainly in the short term, it is unlikely that the new railway will use this location as a passenger facility. *Ken Nunn, Peter Treloar collection/J. F. Bolton, John Keylock collection/MJS*

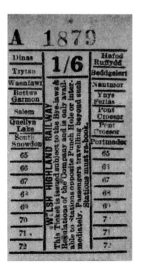

Immediately on continuing its journey southwards from Tryfan Junction, the old railway encountered the junction from which the location received its name. In deference to the traffic that initially originated in the Moel Tryfan quarries, the line to Bryngwyn was identified as the 'main line', whereas the route to and through Waunfawr was known as the branch. In this view of 23 August 1961, the photographer's father stands at the junction, map in hand, wondering which way to go! The track has gone, but the farmer's own track leads to the right along what was the line to Bryngwyn, while the erstwhile 'branch' strikes out behind the intrepid explorer, to the left.

Barely recognisable as the same location, this is approximately the same view on 5 February 2000. The well-used farmer's track is still obvious, but now the left-hand stretch is seeing more usage, with the installation of a metal gate. The foul weather experienced by the restoration gangs is once more amply demonstrated by the condition of the main trackway.

Even more change is apparent as the new railway has faced and surmounted the problem of accommodating the two farm tracks and the requirement of the railway to re-instate one as a permanent way. The solution was to install a dramatically altered layout of the 'junction', with the Bryngwyn line still largely following its well-trodden path (through the gateway straight ahead), while the railway takes over its birthright, and the old left-hand farm access is given a completely new, purpose-built road, accessed over the level crossing to the left, as seen on 2 June 2003. *Sydney Leleux/MJS (2)*

Waunfawr was the terminus for the first phase of the extension southwards from Dinas. On the outskirts of the village, it was not the most important stop on the old railway, but was provided with a fairly substantial stone building in the railway's house style, in keeping with most other stations on the route as far as Rhyd Ddu. This is the view on 23 May 1970, more than 30 years since closure, and, although the upper part of the structure has disappeared, the bulk of the building remains in this isolated location, with the flank of Moel Eilio in the background. The old track ran in front of the face of the building seen here, from bottom centre of the picture into the tree line on the right.

By 5 February 2000 the station building has been dismantled, stone by stone, with the intention of recreation at some future time, and works have begun in earnest to create a new station for the 21st century. The basic rural atmosphere remains, but the 'Snowdonia Parc' public house, on the right, has moved with the times and has provided some amenities for the younger generation. Once again, the atrocious weather conditions in which the gangs were forced to attempt the railway's re-creation can be seen in the lake surrounding the dumper trucks and the mist threatening to shroud Moel Eilio. *John Edgington/MJS*

By 14 July 2000 much progress has been made, despite the weather conditions, and the basic layout of the new island platform can be discerned. Proximity of pub to railway was to be a boon and a source of revenue to both parties – and welcome refreshment for travellers! – as the railway developed.

The date is now 2 June 2003 and the railway is in full operation. While basic facilities have still to be provided at the station, including a waiting shelter, concentration has instead been on providing a railway that functions well and gives the travelling public a smooth and enjoyable ride. Funky diesel *Caernarfon Castle* begins the return trip to Caernarfon, past the newly created grass mound 'boundary' on the left. *Both MJS*

Jumping back 80 years from the last page, the WHR is seen in its early days, as single-Fairlie *Moel Tryfan* pauses at Waunfawr on a sunny 15 May 1923 with the 9.45am Dinas-South Snowdon (Rhyd Ddu) service. Two passengers peer from the single Pickering carriage, while the moustachioed driver stands at the cab door, posing for his portrait. Note the headlamp, ubiquitous sand bucket on the engine's buffer beam, the very interesting, rarely photographed, low wagon behind, and the bridge in the background, with telltale yellow brickwork and from where the views on the previous page were taken.

The relaid railway, with its new island platform arrangement, has perforce not slavishly followed the course of the old line, which was built for a different generation and for vastly different locomotives. This is very roughly the same vantage point on 2 June 2003, as *Caernarfon Castle* runs round its train, before retracing its steps to Dinas and Caernarfon. Note how much higher the bridge is, following groundwork beneath it, compared with the earlier photograph. *Ken Nunn/MJS*

As previously mentioned, the original station building at Waunfawr was dismantled stone by stone, and this undertaking is well under way in this view from 8 September 1999. The intention was to use the material to recreate the station at some future time; however, through whatever circumstances, the stones, although carefully numbered, somehow disappeared, making such a scheme impossible. The elevation and line of the original platform can be seen between the ladder and the pallet, with 'foreman' John Keylock nonchalantly standing on the old trackbed, trademark cigarette in hand.

Though the snow does it best to transform the location, this is the same view on 28 December 2000, with the huddle of humanity standing roughly where the old station building once was. Once upon a time, preserved railways only ran during the summer months, with the possible exception of Santa Specials, but with changing fashions in tourism, the season is now virtually all year round. This leads to yet more headaches for the operations side, as staff and volunteers must be found for an ever-increasing length of season and number of duties.

Although it is now high summer, on 2 June 2003, the sun resolutely refuses to shine; indeed, there is drizzle in the air as *Caernarfon Castle* enters the station, bringing another trainload of passengers who, at this time of day, can enjoy the longer lunchtime turn-round to sample the wares of the adjacent pub! *David Allan/WHR Heritage collection (2)/MJS*

In the first of these two views of the modern station at Waunfawr, taken on 14 July 2000, the basic outline of the emerging island platform can be discerned, with the elemental trackwork laid, right and left, work in hand near the road bridge and a drain in process of being installed in the foreground. Compared to the original NWNGR/WHR station, this new one is self-evidently on a much grander scale, once again more suited to the needs of the travelling public of the 21st century.

By the 5 May 2002 the station is open for business, complete with nameboard, seating and new footbridge access from the pub car-park, complete with period-design lighting at the top of the steps up from the platform. With the attractive and tidy flowerbeds – and even the protective yellow line along the platform edge – the whole is both evidence of the massive amount of hard work from all parties involved in the creation of the new railway, and also a credit to the vision of and provision by those same parties, which in turn enhances the visitor experience. Space exists at the foot of the steps for a waiting shelter in due course. *Both MJS*

Waunfawr was the terminus during this phase of reconstruction, and a run-round was provided at the southern end of the station, not only to give visitors an extra focus, watching the locomotive negotiating the trackwork to run round and reach the other end of its train ready for the return trips, but also provided tantalising glimpses of the mountains in the distance and the promise of what views were to come. On 16 September 2000, old and new rub shoulders in their respective attractive maroon liveries, as *Russell* (from 1906) and *Taliesin* (nearest the camera and 93 years younger, although built by the FR to the period single-Fairlie design in 1999) jointly use the run-round facility, before returning their special celebration train as the 1330 to Caernarfon. Even the engine crews lived up to this comparison, with the younger FR pairing on *Taliesin* outnumbered in years by *Russell*'s more mature driver and fireman – the latter complete with mutton-chop whiskers! *MJS*

HERITAGE
by John Keylock
Secretary and founder member of the WHR Heritage Group

A s I write, four years have passed since the publication of what, with hindsight, must be regarded as Volume 1 on the heritage of the Welsh Highland Railway. It is said that 'history begins yesterday', but the writer must straight away show his hand and declare that his interest focuses mainly on the railway and its predecessors up until closure in 1937. The present is there for all to see, but much of the railway's past is represented by images and 'paperwork'. The railway, since re-opening from Caernarfon, has achieved a high profile and, happily, this fact has to a degree been instrumental in bringing new information into the open. To the historically minded this is 'food and drink' and can but help to elaborate on the 'past' aspect of this publication.

It is accepted that the main purpose for building the North Wales Narrow Gauge Railway – predecessor to the Welsh Highland – was to facilitate transport of slate from the Moel Tryfan and Gwyfrai Valley quarries to Dinas, for transhipment on the LNWR. From Dinas the slate was distributed via the national rail network, or taken to Caernarfon for export by sea. Because the Moel Tryfan quarries were by far the most productive, the line from Dinas to the foot of the Bryngwyn branch was styled 'the main line', the section from Tryfan Junction to Rhyd Ddu being 'the branch'.

Other outward goods were granite setts, iron-ore, empty beer barrels and wool – in season. However, during the period 1913-21 there arose another important traffic – timber from Beddgelert Forest. Since the 1890s there had been a plethora of schemes to continue the railway south from Rhyd Ddu (variously known as Snowdon and South Snowdon) to Beddgelert and Portmadoc, in which latter town a junction with the Festiniog Railway was envisaged. This ultimately came to pass in 1923. However, by 1908 an alignment had been built south from Rhyd Ddu to Pitt's Head and on into Beddgelert Forest. Track was laid under the auspices of the erstwhile Portmadoc, Beddgelert & South Snowdon Railway, which continued as an entity until 1922.

In December 1912 a three-year agreement was drawn up between Thomas Parry – timber merchant of Mold, in Flintshire – and the PB&SSR. This allowed Parry to use the aforementioned track to haul out timber – using horse power – from the estate of one Colonel Parry in Beddgelert Forest. Additional land at Rhyd Ddu was rented for the establishment of a sawmill, and arrangements for transporting the sawn timber to Dinas were made with the NWNGR. Timber extraction continued until at least 1921, production being essentially pit props for use in the coal mines. Bearing in mind that this covered the period of the First World War, one cannot help but speculate on the possibility of timbers being exported to France to shore up the battlefield trenches. Standing in the car park at Rhyd Ddu today, it is difficult to imagine such a hive of activity, in what remains a comparatively remote area. The sawmill was operated by a stationary steam engine, and a Scotch derrick was used to load the processed timber on to the NWNGR wagons. It is interesting to note that for the transport of wool bales from Beddgelert in subsequent years, the favoured wagons were the timber bolsters.

Having considered outward traffic, let us now look at what the complete WHR carried – essentially south from Dinas.

The line served an inherently agricultural and village economy, apart from the slate quarries at Moel Tryfan, for by the mid-1920s mining and quarrying in the Gwyfrai valley had virtually ceased. Furthermore, road transport was coming into greater prominence by this time. Coal represented by far the most important inwards goods, and additional ex-War Department wagons were acquired to cope with this traffic. There were at least eight coal merchants along the line, for at this time virtually every household had a coal fire. The fuel arrived at Dinas by LMS wagonload, where it was transhipped to the narrow gauge – a tedious business of shovelling, for which the coal wholesaler paid 6d per ton! The 'black gold' was also sent up the Bryngwyn incline, for use in the quarry locomotives. Next in bulk were goods to meet the farmers' needs – lime, basic slag and fertilisers (often described on conveyance notes as 'manure'!). Also delivered to the farmers were animal feed, sheep dip and fencing materials.

In the 1920s and '30s the village shop reigned supreme, and today it is difficult to comprehend how many traders there were, for example, in Beddgelert, or even a smaller community like Rhyd Ddu. A major traffic was barrels of beer for the Beddgelert hotels and the Quellyn Arms in Rhyd Ddu. These barrels were invariably 'kils' – an abbreviation for kilderkin – holding 16-18 gallons. Boxes of fish from Grimsby and sides of bacon came to the hotels; boxes of jam to the grocers (jars were returnable); and Lyons cakes were conveyed at a 'pastry scale' rate. Bicycles and motor-cycles came to a dealer in Beddgelert; there were pipes from Portmadoc's Britannia Foundry; cement, timber, furniture, carpets, china and seeds. Snowdonia being a holiday destination, there was also considerable PLA traffic – 'passengers luggage in advance' – which took the form of trunks, tents and suitcases.

The arrival of all these goods was meticulously documented and, of course, their carriage had to be paid for. Heavy goods were charged at a tonnage rate and the consignee would generally have an account with the railway company. The cost of conveying small packages was indicated to the customer by the application of parcel stamps. Goods other than coal had to be delivered, and this service was contracted out to a local haulier, certainly at Beddgelert, which was the major centre of population between Dinas and Portmadoc.

But most important of all, perhaps, were the people who made the service work. The stationmaster at Dinas shared his time between the WHR and LMS, and it was his unenviable task to try and sort out which railway was responsible for any breakages in transit! There was a daily early morning freight to Bryngwyn, consisting of loaded coal wagons and slate empties. The passenger train to Beddgelert – a sort of railway frontier, where passengers changed trains for Portmadoc – usually consisted of three coaches, one of which had a guards/goods compartment. The best known – and most photographed – engine drivers were 'Willie Hugh' Williams and Goronwy Roberts. The former worked for the railway in NWNGR days, while Goronwy graduated from being a stoker (fireman). Daffyd Lloyd Hughes was a guard of long standing on both goods and passenger trains. Drivers' logs give a fascinating insight into train operation.

After opening in 1923 and initial success with passenger traffic, revenue quickly declined and with it the staffing of the more important, intermediate stations. Beddgelert's first stationmaster was another Mr Jones, who cycled to work – for this he received an allowance

At Dinas on 18 July 1941 are both standard and narrow gauge freight wagons, showing the unloading arrangement in the yard. Goods could be unloaded from the former to the latter by gravity, from such as the five-, six- and seven-plank, 10T wooden or 12T steel LMS wagons, to the all-wooden narrow gauge versions, like Nos 2 and 4, below; the reverse operation was handled by narrow gauge wagons being shunted on to an elevated track, to bring them to the same body height as their standard gauge companions. The LMS types are certainly in better operational condition. *H. C. Casserley*

of 1 shilling per week! His requisitions for material to run the station – and oil to lubricate the coaches and wagons – likewise make for fascinating reading. He was constantly under pressure to gather in monies outstanding to the railway. He also distributed timetable handbills promoting the railway around the village, but, alas, the motorbus was gaining ascendancy. Beddgelert's bus operator had done a journey to Portmadoc and back before the arrival of the first train of the day!

By 1927 the WHR was in receivership under Colonel Stephens, who had come to the railway as engineer and manager at the outset. It was he who purchased the additional bogie coal wagons, as well as en ex-WD 4-6-0 Baldwin locomotive. Always with an eye for a bargain, he also acquired a number of 'toast-rack' carriages from Hudson's of Leeds. At the time of writing, one of these is in the final stages of rebuilding at Gelert's Farm, Porthmadog. In 1928 one half of a carriage was converted for use as a 'Buffet Car'. Advertised as being licensed, there remains no proof that it was, apart from the involvement of a local hotelier!

And so the railway struggled on, with a restricted service in which 'summer' was a mere three months, from July to September. Imagine the success of today's tourist-orientated railways if they adopted a similar strategy! The year 1930 represented the nadir of the railway's (mis)fortunes, and in 1934 the Festiniog Railway took a lease on the undertaking. In an attempt to attract customers, the carriages were painted in gaudy colours and a 'Five Valleys Tour' was re-introduced. Newly painted they may have been, but the carriages did not enhance passenger comfort! However, against all odds, passenger figures did return to levels achieved in the mid-1920s and, fortunately for the historian, many photographs of the railway, and its locomotives in particular, were taken in the last two years of passenger operation, 1935/6.

In 14 years of life (1923-36) the WHR carried a mere 230,000 passengers, of whom 1,331 elected to use the First Class option. It is interesting to note that the modest WHR operation based at Gelert's Farm in Porthmadog has already been 'up and running' longer than its historical counterpart! WHR freight ceased in 1937, after which the Baldwin and Russell locomotives languished in Dinas engine shed, with the carriages parked outside until sold.

So what remains? Two bogie carriages on the FR and the 'Gladstone' coach at Gelert's Farm, so named from having been used by the then Prime Minister, to travel from Dinas to Rhyd Ddu, en route to stay with friends in Nant Gwynant. Also at Gelert's Farm, awaiting restoration, is the buffet car and, of course, that most charismatic and historically important of narrow gauge locomotives – *Russell*. Currently out of service for general overhaul, it is due back in service for 'his' centenary in 2006.

Besides the paperwork – of which much more is in prospect – and rolling-stock, there are many more remains still extant. Such items of infrastructure still with us today inevitably stem from the NWNGR, whose buildings were rather more substantial than the WHR's timber and corrugated iron structures. At Dinas there is the original goods shed and the restored and

As will be seen elsewhere, the WHR's side-tank locomotive No 12 *Russell* was the mainstay of operations right up to closure in 1937. In this view at Dinas on 8 August 1935 there appears no hint of any problem with the railway, with *Russell* looking in very good condition and LMS wagons waiting for their next duties. Note the cut-out in the cab roof and 'truncated' dome and chimney, necessary to meet the lower loading gauge on the FR. *H. F. Wheeller, Roger Carpenter collection*

award-winning station building. Tryfan Junction station building, long hidden beneath rampant undergrowth, is currently being worked on to prevent further dilapidation, with the hope of eventual rebuilding. The remains of Betws Garmon station survive, immediately to the north of the new river bridge, as does the shell of the weigh-house adjacent to the line at the foot of Glanrafon quarry.

Many road overbridges remain, albeit some in modified form to enable compliance with current rail – and road – requirements and standards. Railway construction was much more plain-sailing in the 1880s – and, indeed, the 1920s – but today's brave 'new' railway is built to a far more demanding specification. Just south of Beddgelert, as one travels by road to Porthmadog, is an overbridge built in 1905 by the PB&SSR that came to nothing – but that is another story! And still there is more to be savoured of the WHR – or, more precisely, the NWNGR – than the tangible remaining artefacts and documents so beloved of and kept safely by the historically minded – the raison d'être of the railway's original promotion, the tips of slate waste. It must be remembered that for every 100 tons of slate quarried, no more than 10% was a saleable commodity. Particularly between Waenfawr and Rhyd Ddu, these cascades of slate waste on the mountainsides have become part of the landscape, the most prominent being at Glanrafon. In some instances, the remains of inclines are also apparent. One never ceases to marvel at the Victorian ingenuity for accessing minerals in relatively inaccessible places – but so often resulting in bankruptcy!

The Bryngwyn 'branch' was the prime reason for the original railway, bringing slates down the incline from the complex of quarries on Moel Tryfan for movement to Dinas. At the time of writing, half of the trackbed on the 'branch' is designated as a permissive footpath, but hopefully the other half – to Tryfan Junction – will be similarly utilised ere long.

So – a new Welsh Highland has come, but, thankfully, so much of the original still remains.

Freight from the WHR: empty beer barrels for Burton (*opposite below*), wool destined for Halifax (*opposite bottom*), and slate to Birmingham (*right*).

Three examples of the WHR's freight stock, all seen at Dinas on 8 August 1935 and all scrapped five years later! Road Van No 2 (*below left*) looks to have seen some recent refurbishment as it stands in company with later-numbered items of goods wagons. The livery at this time was crimson lake, with black ironwork and white-stencilled letters and numbers. At the end of the same line is five-plank coal wagon No 12 (*below right*); note the siding leading to the higher level in the background. Confusingly, there was also a covered van numbered 2 (see also page 38), seen here (*bottom*) with 'sister' No 4, both with corrugated iron sheeted roofs that had replaced the originals some time earlier. Some of Dinas's sparse housing looks to have been fairly recently built in this view. *All H. F. Wheeller, Roger Carpenter collection*

CONSIGNMENT NOTE. No. 77   Date, 8 Ap   192 8

From the AMALGAMATED SLATE ASSOCIATION, Limited.
TO THE NORTH WALES NARROW GAUGE RAILWAYS COMPANY.

Please receive and forward Slate as follows, to Soho Pool:
L. M. rs Ry

Postal address Broadbent & Stephens.

Wagon No.	Size.	Quantity.	Quality.	Weight			Who Pays Carriage.
				T	C.	Q.	
57	24 x 12	475	S.B		7	1	Paid to Dinas
"	22 x 12	235	"	18	2		Junction
"	22 x 11	235	"	11	0		
33	20 x 12	475	"	1	2	2	
"	20 x 10	475	"	16	3		
21	18 x 12	475	"	18	3		120581
"	18 x 10	475	"	15	3		
38	16 x 12	235	"	8	0		
"	14 x 12	475	"	14	1		
				7	5	0	

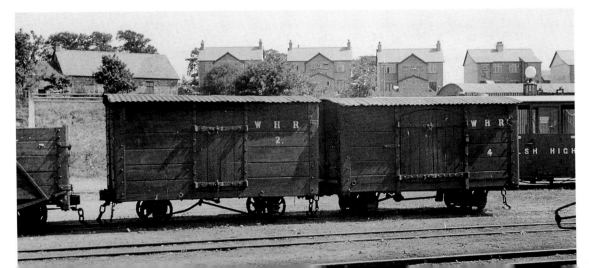

As John Keylock mentions in his text, in the 1930s the FR attempted to boost flagging interest and revenue by painting WHR coaches in a variety of colours, and re-introducing the 'Five Valley Circular Tour (*left*). Red, green and yellow are seen at Rhyd Ddu in 1936 (*below*), as Guard Dafydd Lloyd Hughes clings to the open window slots of the end coach, teetering along the narrow running board. *Russell* stands patiently at the head of the train, awaiting the 'right away' for the return trip to Dinas. *MJS collection*

Top and middle Traffic and timetable problems in the 1920s.

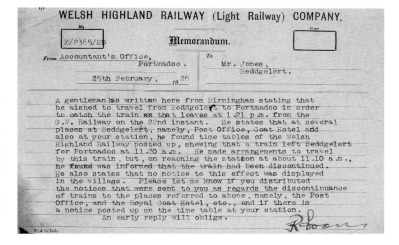

FESTINIOG RAILWAY.

Memorandum.

My M/733/TR

From Portmadoc

To Stationmaster Beddgelert

Octr 19th 19 23

(113)

Porter

Re my letter of the 8th inst. Owing to the very small passen-ger traffic on the W.H.Rly it has been decided to curtail the train service from 1st Novr so that the Stationmaster only will be required in charge there. You had better tell Lewis Parry Jones that we shall not require his services after today and you may enter him 10/- in next pay for this week.

I will write you again regarding Porter T.J.Williams.

(W. & S. Ltd.)

WELSH HIGHLAND RAILWAY (Light Railway) COMPANY.

Memorandum.

My E/2365/ED

From Accountant's Office, Portmadoc.

To Mr. Jones, Beddgelert.

25th February, 19 26

A gentleman has written here from Birmingham stating that he wished to travel from Beddgelert to Portmadoc in order to catch the train on that leaves at 1.21 p.m. from the G.W. Railway on the 22nd instant. He states that at several places at Beddgelert, namely, Post Office, Goat Hotel and also at your station, he found time tables of the Welsh Highland Railway posted up, shewing that a train left Beddgelert for Portmadoc at 11.20 a.m. He made arrangements to travel by this train, but, on reaching the station at about 11.10 a.m., he found was informed that the train had been discontinued. He also states that no notice to this effect was displayed in the village. Please let me know if you distributed the notices that were sent to you as regards the discontinuance of trains to the places referred to above, namely, the Post Office, and the Royal Goat Hotel, etc., and if there is a notice posted up on the time table at your station.

An early reply will oblige.

W. & S. Ltd.

Below No 4 is a Guard's Brake Composite, in original condition, with full-height roof and Westinghouse brake. Built in 1907 by R. Y. Pickering & Co Ltd, it was altered around 1923, with a new set of cast steel wheels and the roof reduced in height and re-covered, for use within the FR loading gauge. Note the segregation of First and Third Class. *Historical Model Railway Society collection*

Above This is the same vehicle after alteration and with the addition of cast lettering picked out in white paint. Once again, the view is at Dinas, by the impressive goods shed, and the date is 8 August 1935. Note the destination board, midway along the cantrail, and that vacuum braking has also been provided. *H. F. Wheeller, Roger Carpenter collection*

Below Next along the train on the same day, one of the railway's two 1893-vintage Ashbury Railway Carriage & Iron Co Ltd 'Corridor Coaches' stands at Dinas, with two ladies apparently being the only occupants for the trip to Beddgelert. The 'Gladstone' coach on the left is attached at the rear of the train. *H. F. Wheeller, Roger Carpenter collection*

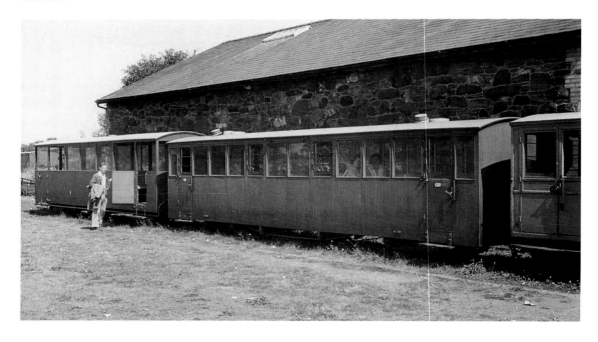

THE ROUTE PAST AND PRESENT: WAUNFAWR TO RHYD DDU

The headshunt featured on page 36 is seen again, but this time looking from the south back towards Waunfawr station on 5 December 2000. The comparison between the muddy foreground and the area ballasted and tracked graphically demonstrates both how much has been achieved and how much tidier the finished product looks against the state of the trackbed before work starts in earnest in this more open stretch of the line.

Less than a year later, the whole ambience is very different – and not merely because the sun is shining! As can be seen, work has carried on apace and track now forges towards Betws Garmon, site of the next station on the original line. To assist with the work, especially transporting heavier items, *Upnor Castle* was moved from the FR and is seen in its two-tone green livery on 12 October 2001, resting at the northern extent of its territory at this stage. The then still current headshunt can be glimpsed in the background, with access still barred between the two at this stage. *David Allan, WHR Heritage collection/MJS*

Above As has already been seen, the railway has had to accommodate farmers and other neighbours as it progresses along the proposed route. This has meant remedial attention to bridges both under and over the line, and to level crossings and access points; one such is superbly exemplified here as one of the railway's neighbours prepares to cross the line on his new access path on 12 October 2001. The bright yellow vintage tractor, from the farm buildings in the background, sits well with the heritage nature of the railway in the landscape. *MJS*

Left Turning through 180 degrees on the same day, and moving closer to Betws Garmon station site, this is the view ahead. The half-laid track points the way towards the bulk of Elephant Mountain and, in the distant tree-line, the much nearer road bridge on the outskirts of the village of Betws Garmon. The clump of trees in the centre of the picture shields what still remains of the old station building, which the railway will pass to the left, on a gentle left-hand curve on the approach to the river bridge immediately after the station site. *MJS*

Restoration progress was continually frustrated by structures and obstacles. One major stumbling block was the bridge over the River Gwyrfai at Betws Garmon, seen in the foreground of this view on 12 April 2000, as an intrepid visitor apparently ignores the 'Danger' sign to cross the river on the parapet of the old bridge. As Dave Kent explained earlier, this original structure would not suffice for the future and was replaced by a wider and stronger one, just over three years after this shot. The road bridge briefly mentioned opposite is seen here straight ahead, taking the Waunfawr-Beddgelert road over the trackbed.

Some idea of the lengthened span – witness the boulders on the water's edge – and more substantial support for the new bridge are well highlighted in this view of the yawning gap on 1 June 2003. The substantial stone-faced concrete cradles for the new bridge may look 'out of scale', but will be necessary for a much heavier bridge than the original. Note the new road bridge, recently introduced by the local authorities, complete with more substantial retaining walls, and the looming presence of Elephant Mountain in the background of both views. *David Allan, WHR Heritage collection/MJS*

47

The classic and attractive shape of the original bridge is clearly seen in this view from the south on 23 May 1970. The bow bridges were a feature of the original line, and it would have been more desirable to retain this for the new railway, but sadly the condition of both bridge and river at this point precluded such a happy outcome.

Again, the updated requirements for the new structure are obvious from this comparative view, taken on 1 June 2003. The new design effectively gave a bed to the newly provided bridge, the leading edge of which can just be glimpsed on the extreme left – so near and yet so far!

Four days later there are sighs of relief all round, as the bridge has been lowered into position, without a hitch, fitting snugly into place at the first attempt and within millimetres of the designed specification! Contractors, railway Directors and other supporters savour their first sight of the new facility and think ahead to the future sight of trains running over it. *John Edgington/MJS (2)*

A last look at the old bridge – again on a sunny 23 May 1970 – looking north to the Betws Garmon station site, with the remains of the old building just visible above the left-hand bow. The trackbed is sprouting young trees!

The three Mikes – left to right, Whitehouse (Chairman, Ffestiniog Railway Company and WHLR), Schumann (Director, FR Company and Trustee, FR Trust) and Hart (Director, FR Company) – wear happy and satisfied expressions, moments after the bridge is safely in place on 5 June 2003. The chains are still attached, but the re-engineered structure sits securely on its new foundations – a credit to all concerned, not least the Welsh Highland Railway Society for providing the finance. Note the provision of mesh walkways either side of the central trackbed behind them. *John Edgington/MJS*

Left The view ahead on 1 June 2003, under the road bridge at Betws Garmon, towards the railhead and passing Bryn Gloch Caravan Park, shows the reinforced track base under the bridge and the work needed to bring the approaching trackbed up to the same level. Once more, as seen in previous photographs, the shoulder of Elephant Mountain peers into view on the right. Following the opening of the railway in August 2003, trains were constantly saluted by happy, waving campers as they rounded the left-hand curve ahead. *MJS*

This page Happily, the bow bridge at Plas-y-nant, south of Betws Garmon, is still in situ and serviceable for the new railway. Long shrouded by trees and bushes, it was still just visible from the nearby road on 10 October 2001, showing the watercourse underneath and the makeshift access walkway across it, installed by a local resident.

By the time of the second view, 1 June 2003, there has evidently been much clearance, as progress has now reached the level of rails back on the bridge (albeit with a short-term stop immediately after) and the provision of an alternative walkway for that resident at the far side of the bridge. The bridge, too, has been the recipient of much 'TLC' and looks rejuvenated in its new grey coat. In the distance, the track gang are on site to further the work on underlying formation and consideration of the approach to the bridge from the south. *Both MJS*

Having left the road and accessed the trackbed by way of the small iron gate on the extreme right, this is the view of that bridge from the southern approach, on 23 May 1970. Effectively abandoned, the trees are beginning to take hold and the timbers on the bridge bed are slowing rotting.

By 5 June 1995 the trees have gained ground, invading the trackbed, the timbers are rapidly disappearing and there is now the first sign of a plank to provide foot access for that local neighbour. Other than the bridge itself, there is no other evidence that a railway ever ran here.

A true transformation! Not only has the bridge been completely renovated and prepared for the heavyweight trains, but the railway has shown its good-neighbourliness by providing a grand, purpose-built foot access, now to the left-hand side of the bridge, to keep human from machine! Note how close the road is to the railway, on the right, and that the old gate has disappeared.
John Edgington/MJS (2)

Turning round to face south, the ever-present Elephant is seen again, to the right, as the ongoing trackbed is photographed on 12 October 2001. Not that the uninitiated would regard this apparently open field as such, apart from the possible giveaway fencing to the left. The old route here is straight as a die towards the mountain, before kicking left along the far tree line.

Once more the transformation is dramatic. The view on 1 June 2003 shows how much progress has been made and confirms to even the most myopic that a railway is preparing to re-invade the territory. Note how space has been provided on the left of the trackbed – and a point put in place – to facilitate the re-creation of the halt that once stood here – although, hopefully, a little more substantial than of yore! Residents have expressed an interest in such a facility, which, hopefully, will in turn aid the success of the railway. *Both MJS*

That deviation from the straight, to avoid the shoulder of the mountain, is seen here from the other end, at Castell Cidwm, as the trackbed prepares to once again dive under the A4085 roadway. The works at Plas-y-nant, seen on the last few pages, are to the right of this view and we are beginning to enter the more rugged stretch of the journey to Rhyd Ddu. In this view from the late 1960s, only occasional feet troubled the long-dormant trackbed.

As Dave Kent explained earlier, the extension was restored from several locations at the same time, rather than a linear process. While this was largely caused by the sheer logistics of accessing the trackbed itself, there were occasions where local opposition did not assist. This location was a case in point: the railway was denied direct access across neighbouring land, so had to complete tracklaying from either end of this cutting, delaying the final completion. However, where there's a will... This is the view of final preparations, before track can be laid, on 2 June 2003. Note that, once again, drainage has been an important consideration. *Jon Marsh/MJS*

Crossing over the road, this the view looking south at Castell Cidwm, with the lofty peak of Snowdon dominating the central horizon and reinforcing the promise of spectacular views on this stretch of the new railway. On 23 May 1970 the site that was once Old Quellyn station and a temporary NWNGR terminus here lies undisturbed, with the trackbed showing evidence of access by four-wheeled vehicles.

The rails have stopped short some distance from the road bridge, due to opposition from a local landowner, but preparations are well under way on 2 June 2003 for the eventual return of metals to this section and completion of the route to Rhyd Ddu, with a much tidier appearance to the shallow cutting's slopes. *John Edgington/MJS*

This page And so we reach Snowdon Ranger/Quellyn Lake station – not that you would know it from this shot! What appears to be merely a clothes-line, is in fact an appropriation of the old station nameboard posts, and the old trackbed, just to the right of the posts, would have been close enough for the towels to wipe the coach sides! With Llyn Cwellyn in the background, this is the view on 23 August 1961.

Four years later, on 24 July 1965, the posts are seen again on the right, close to the old station building, now a private residence. Note that the old trackbed is still visible, with the original low platform still discernible immediately in front of the building, a secluded 'bijou residence' at this time. The northern outpost of Beddgelert Forest rises in the background, with telegraphic posts marching uphill.

With the residence now obviously valuing its privacy, the new railway has had to veer slightly away from the original formation – the former line was virtually at the foot of the current hedge. A new station was being built some 100 yards to the left of this view on 2 June 2003, but not ready for use for passengers in the very short term. *Sydney Leleux/ Michael Bishop/MJS*

Opposite page Walking past the now private old station building, this is the vista in the late 1950s before a bungalow was built alongside, to the left. Note that the trackbed still visible, together with the stone base of the old water tank tower in the foreground, strategically placed for replenishing locomotives en route.

With the roof of the new bungalow peeping over the hedge on the left, the previously open vantage point has now an enclosed feel, as work continues in making the trackbed ready for the rails. On 2 June 2003 this short stretch is devoid of metal, to allow access for machinery in connection with the building of the new Snowdon Ranger station. Once opened, it will give excellent travelling opportunities for walkers wishing to access one of the walks to Snowdon's summit. *David Lawrence, Hugh Davies collection/MJS*

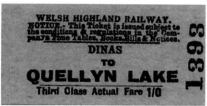

WELSH HIGHLAND RAILWAY.
NOTICE.- This Ticket is issued subject to
the conditions & regulations in the Com-
pany's Time Tables, Books, Bills & Notices.
DINAS
TO
QUELLYN LAKE
Third Class Actual Fare 1/0
1393

We are now a further 250 yards or so along the trackbed towards Rhyd Ddu, with the new bungalow at the former station site just visible in the distance. To the left is Snowdon Ranger Hostel, open to the public as a hotel in a previous incarnation. While the old trackbed is even more obvious here, on 18 March 1998, its condition for restoration is somewhat questionable, as it is less than uniform or solid. Note the base of an old signal, just visible as a wooden stump immediately above the stone slab at the foot of the picture.

On 2 June 2003 the railway presence has again totally transformed the old formation. Now there are rails, drainage and a sense of order, and even with storm clouds looming there is a revitalised landscape. The stone wall on the right remains, but the fencing has been replaced on the left, while elsewhere the countryside goes about its natural leafy business. *David Allan, WHR Heritage collection/MJS*

Now looking south from the same vantage point, the old trackbed heads away and disappears into the distance, lost among grass and fields at the foot of the abandoned slate heaps of Glanrafon Quarry in the middle distance. Note how, on this day in March 1998, the boundary walls have seen much better days, their condition no doubt helped by the passage of many sheep's hoofs! Pre-foot and mouth sheep graze lazily on the left-hand hillside.

By 2 June 2003, the walls are not much better, but now there is newly erected fencing to protect both animals and railway. Once again, the clean lines of the new track contrast with the less formal nature of the surroundings, as it heads towards the very threatening clouds smothering the peak of Snowdon. *David Allan, WHR Heritage collection/MJS*

Sheep may safely graze, they say, but in mid-afternoon on a bright April day in 1962 so may a horse on the trackbed, free from disturbance by dangerous machines! The view here is further on towards Rhyd Ddu, looking back towards Snowdon Ranger, with Llyn Cwellyn to the left, beyond the road that here runs roughly parallel with the line of the trackbed. Once more, the imperious flanks of Elephant Mountain rise above the landscape.

Forty-odd years later the day is not so sunny – indeed, your photographer was threatened by an oncoming deluge – but the left-hand mountainside is far clearer than in the haze above, as is the line of the railway, pinpointed by the clean ballast and thus far rusty rails, as yet virgin to service trains. Fencing has again sprouted to protect the railway and there are other subtle changes, such as the retention of the solitary tree by the middle-distance wall, while its former neighbours have been grubbed out. *Michael Davies/MJS*

By far the most substantial structure on this part of the railway is Glanrafon 'Viaduct', a lofty bridge situated between Snowdon Ranger and a point just north of the quarry sidings site to be visited shortly. Some 60 feet above the gorge carved by the Afon Treweunydd, it is an impressive location, but one sadly virtually inaccessible by foot below and totally unappreciated from the new railway, due to the growth of surrounding trees and vegetation. In this view from the northern end, in July 1963, a party of railway enthusiasts risk life and limb to give the structure closer examination.

The view from the southern approach, 40 years later, on 1 June 2003, amply demonstrates the restricted view due to the trees, but also shows progress in returning the line to working status. Gone are the narrow trackbed and curved handrails, to be replaced by a wider structure with supporting cross-beams. The first new timbers lay ready for the rest of the preparation for relaying the rails and the fitting of a wire mesh walkway on either side of the tracks. It is instructive to consider that the railway was fully relaid and formally opened by the Prince of Wales less than two months after this view! *Nick Booker/MJS*

Above The view south, with Snowdon Ranger now well behind us, shows Glanrafon Quarry sidings. The ruts of the old sleepers are still readily visible on both the 'main line', on the right, and a siding to the left. Part of the remaining slate waste heap can be seen top left, and the processed material would have arrived at the sidings from the workings high up on the hillside by way of an incline. Material would then have been weighed on a weighbridge, controlled from the building still extant in this view from Whitsun 1964. A small party of early WHR supporters review the scene in the midday heat. *Nick Booker*

Opposite page These two views show development of the railway on the final run to Rhyd Ddu. On 31 October 2001, with access some distance away, the dumper truck negotiates a slippery, slate-strewn trackbed, battling against prevailing weather conditions to effect the necessary remedial steps for the arrival of the new railway. New fencing has appeared on both sides, but elsewhere there is little evidence of the prospective railway.

A little over six months later, on 12 May 2002, progress is obvious. The sweeping curve and metal sleepers clearly mark out the way forward, and visitors Michael Davies, Cedric Lodge and Derek Lyster all look pleased with progress. It is interesting to compare these two views with those on page 27 of Volume 1, showing the same location in earlier times. *Both David Allan, WHR Heritage collection*

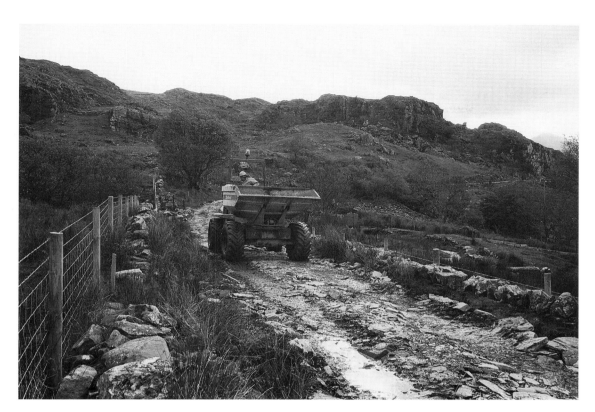

Llyn Cwellyn

We are now on the final approaches to Rhyd Ddu, as the route treads a careful path between the valley below and the rising mountainsides above. With Llyn Cwellyn again vying for centre stage and looking for all the world like a remnant of the Ice Age, the track curves sinuously around boulder and bluff and between protective dry stone walls. A deserted road along the valley floor can just be seen in the centre, echoing the course of the railway in this open, uninterrupted scene from the mid-1920s.

The ensuing years saw railway abandonment and track ripped up, before the new vision was brought into being and the past re-created. In the early evening of a dull 1 June 2003, the light is beginning to fade, but the restoration is both obvious and incredibly successful, with only the growth of vegetation during the past 80 years disguising anything of the earlier view.

The third view is not from exactly the same vantage point, but it is the same stretch of line. On 14 September 2003 Garratt No 143, with steam to spare, makes an impressive sight at the head of a mixed train of ballast wagons and coaches, forming the 0945 Dinas-Rhyd Ddu photographers' special during the railway's 'Super Power Weekend' celebrations. *Peter Johnson collection/MJS, with permission (2)*

In the years leading up to the re-opening of the line to Rhyd Ddu, there were many events to drum up support and/or sell the idea of the restoration. Not least among the proponents was Dave Kent, Chairman of the Welsh Highland Railway Society. On 14 July 1999 he gave a guided walk along the trackbed from Rhyd Ddu to Glanrafon 'Viaduct', with dull and threatening conditions overhead and often waterlogged, boggy ground underfoot. There was a healthy contingent of hardy souls, however, interested in learning more, here being given an introductory talk at Fridd Isaf curve before setting off along the route.

The 'Super Power Weekend' of 14 September 2003 is again seen, showing off the curve to good advantage as the train seen opposite makes its way around the horseshoe, on the very last stretch before the station at Rhyd Ddu. The northern edge of the village can be seen in the background. *Both MJS, with permission*

This page The horseshoe curve at Fridd Isaf is seen again, but now from the other direction, looking back towards Glanrafon. On 14 July 1999 the curve is obvious in the foreground, but disappears into scrub as the route travels away from us, and apart from the shallow stone embankment in the foreground, supporting the formation, there is little to say that it was other than a footpath.

By 12 October 2001 there has been movement and early preparatory work, but other than the new fencing, again any indication of this being a former railway is not blindingly obvious!

The third view is a sight that would have gladdened the hearts of WHR officials in the 1920s/'30s! Motive power with the true power to deal with the demands of this undulating and magnificent railway is provided by the ex-South African Garratts, here seen again during the 'Super Power Weekend', with No 138 *Millennium* bringing up the rear of the 1610 Rhyd Ddu-Dinas service, headed by black-liveried No 143. Now the course of the railway and its horseshoe curvature here are clear. *All MJS*

Opposite page At first sight this view of the final curve into Rhyd Ddu station looks to be part of the new railway of the 21st century, but appearances are deceptive. The vintage 1934 Austin 7 might have been positioned to give a genuine 'heritage' feel to the works, but this is in fact 24 July 1965 and the preparatory ballast and rails belong to the erstwhile '64 Company, as they pondered the best way to re-establish the Welsh Highland presence.

Now we are into the new century, but note how the new railway has had to make a deviation from the original route. The presence of a National Park car park on the original trackbed, at the site of the old station, has meant that the new WHR has had to create a new path around the obstacle. This led to the blasting out of a new course past the large rock near the house seen in both views; the old line was to the right, here occupied by the car, but it now runs to the left. *Michael Bishop/MJS*

The train has arrived safely at Rhyd Ddu, but not everyone, apparently, is happy to be captured by the photographer! A woman rushes towards the station building, trying to escape, as *Russell* pauses for travellers to disembark some time between 1934 and 1936. Elsewhere, plus-fours, short trousers and school cap, and a teenager with a flat cap all point to the era. Note how the cut-out was necessary on *Russell's* cab, as the fireman looks back along the train, and the barred windows on the lead Pickering coach. *Neville Stead collection*

Rhyd Ddu was originally called Snowdon (later South Snowdon), obviously in an attempt to attract walkers and/or sightseers to the mountain. The station nameboard is clearly visible in this 1922 view of a single-Fairlie arriving with a train from Dinas, the waiting passengers casually draped around the station building, with no apparent excitement at the train's appearance! Note the abandoned wagon in the foreground, the leading coach still bearing the NWNGR 'heraldic device', and the furthest building of the station trio proudly announcing 'Refreshment Bar'. The main building is adorned with advertisements for 'Everybody's Tea' (at '2/- a lb'), Allman's Self-Raising Flour and a local brand of 'Bitter'. A healthy fire is evident in the middle building, totally outshining the arriving locomotive!

On 2 June 2003 the old trackbed is now an unmade roadway, giving access to both the house seen on page 67 – just visible in the right distance – and Fridd Isaf, home of Dave and Gina Kent and their 'non-smoking' B&B at the foot of Snowdon. *Rail Archive Stephenson, MJS collection/MJS*

The period is now 1939. The railway has only been out of use for two years, but time has obviously not served the area well. The station nameboard, now proclaiming 'South Snowdon', remains and the walls have had all poster displays altered from the view on the previous page, but these are now devoid of information. The pointwork in the foreground will not be operating again for service trains and the whole has an air of dereliction.

By the mid-1960s abandonment is complete, with the tracks and all of the railway buildings long gone. The dull, damp weather compounds the depressing scene, looking north. The house in the centre is that seen on previous pages, with the path to Snowdon – and the current access to the Kents' B&B – passing through the gate on the right.

Another 40 years has seen relatively little change at this point, apart from the growth of trees and the acceptance of the old trackbed as a roadway, leading to the re-routing of the railway to reach a new station by passing to the right of the distant car.
Photomatic, WHR collection/John Keylock collection/MJS

A final look at the station at Rhyd Ddu from the north. The FR is helping out with motive power and one of the diminutive England saddle-tanks prepares to run round its train, while a young family group wait at this end. Seen on an unidentified Saturday in 1925, this is one of the Caernarfon Market Specials run by the WHR in an attempt to drum up custom. The experiment began on 3 March of that year; this could well be shortly thereafter, and the train is likely to have been the 11.55am from Dinas, arriving at South Snowdon (Rhyd Ddu) at 12.47. Returning to Dinas at 1.00pm, this then gave shoppers plenty of time to find their way to Caernarfon and spend their money. The last return trip from Dinas was at 7.49pm, arriving at South Snowdon at 8.35. Note the totally open vista in this period, with the view through to Llyn-y-Gadair unobstructed, and the two railway 'officials', who appear to be discussing some point between loco and coaches.

On 14 July 2000 the view to the lake has disappeared, the open ambience immeasurably altered by the tree growth. The trackbed-cum-road can be seen, off limits to the new railway.

The new terminus was laid out in the field to the left of the previous view, and on 14 September 2003 the trains are back! Once more seen during the 'Super Power Weekend', Garratt No 143 stands at the head of what will be the 1610 return trip to Dinas. No 138 is at the far end, with the route on to Beddgelert beckoning in the distance. *Mowat collection/MJS/ Tammy Stretton*

THE '64 COMPANY:
AN UPDATE
by David Allan
Chairman, Welsh Highland Railway (Porthmadog)

Perceived wisdom was that all the fireworks and all the action was taking place at the Caernarfon end of the new line. However, this wasn't quite true, for down at Porthmadog the Welsh Highland Railway (Porthmadog) Ltd, formerly the '64 Company, was making steady progress. As was seen in Volume 1, this was the company that back in 1964 was responsible for starting the whole impossible restoration project. Early disagreements were outlined in that volume, but, happily, the somewhat prickly past relationship with the FR was almost completely smoothed out and once again constructive conversation was taking place between the David and the Goliath of the Welsh Highland reconstruction scheme. While the WHR(P) Ltd had vowed to remain robustly independent of its larger neighbour, it nevertheless was now very much a part of the overall plan. Its role was to reconstruct the line from its existing limit at Pen-y-Mount to the delightful river crossing of Pont Croesor. Its

The pride of the fleet! On 13 August 1989, 1906-vintage *Russell* – the sole surviving NWNGR/WHR locomotive – slides out of the platform to start another journey from the Gelert's Farm terminus in Porthmadog, bound for the current destination of Pen-y-Mount, keeping the spirit of the old railway alive and providing a short moment of nostalgia for the visitor. Note the standard-gauge Cambrian Coast line to the left. *Tom Heavyside*

chosen method was to go down the time-honoured route of using mainly volunteer labour. However, an additional layer of bureaucracy had been added to the equation, in the form of the Ffestiniog-led Welsh Highland Construction Company. As the principal contractor, with ultimate responsibility for construction work, it rightly insisted on the dotting of every 'i' and the crossing of every 't'. This was how the new legislation worked and there was no question but that the approved formulae had to be followed.

The first step had been to seek planning approval from the local authority, Gwynedd. However, as in the north, this involved an environmental survey to determine the flora and fauna that may be affected by the building process. A topographical survey was also needed to help with the civil engineering work. The route of a public footpath had to be considered, and finally the appearance of any structures had to be approved. All this was a far cry from those early days of railway reconstruction when the main objective was to get the tracks down as soon as possible!

A further limiting factor was that the funds had to come from members and from well-wishers. The Legal Agreement with the FR specifically rejected any fund-raising activity associated with grant aid, so as not to compete with the FR's activities in that direction. Without much fuss the small team of extension-minded volunteers relentlessly pursued all this essential preliminary activity. Practical work could not start until planning permission had been granted, although some limited gorse clearance was allowed to assist in gaining access to the land for the surveys. Planning permission was finally granted on 17 March 2003.

The team leader had drawn up a detailed plan of campaign and this was implemented. Gangs set to work with a will on the initial 100-yard section between the temporary terminus of Pen y Mount and Cynfal cottage. This section had been used as a dumping ground for over half a century and years of accumulated rubbish had to be cleared and removed by a succession of skips. Gradually, from this gorse and bramble-shrouded strip, the old trackbed formation slowly re-emerged. Though it had not seen a train since 1937, somehow, to the willing workers, it still retained all the drama and romance of a railway line. Unlike the contractor-led work in the north, where time, linked to the Millennium Commission grant, was of the essence, here the emphasis was on getting the most from the limited funds available. Machines were hired and the volunteer operators gained certificates of competence that enabled them to work to the rigorous Health & Safety standards currently demanded.

Once the gorse had been cleared, the next step was to fence the land and re-profile the old formation. The topsoil was stripped off and a layer of slate waste laid down and consolidated. This was to be the basis on which the new ballast would be laid and would also facilitate easy access for road vehicles to get to the far end of the track (see Dave Kent's earlier comments).

A locomotive that looks the part – when fully clothed! – is here receiving attention. The third steam locomotive to be put back in harness at Gelert's Farm, in 1991, Bagnall 0-4-2T *Gelert* stands in the Works yard on 30 June 2003, looking in fine condition and only waiting to be re-united with its tanks before returning to service after a three-year lay-off. *David Allan*

It had already been decided to build and open to Pont Croesor in two stages. The first stage was to a temporary loop at what was variously known as Portreuddyn Loop or Traeth Mawr Halt. This first part was just about three-quarters of a mile in length and would give both passengers and crew a taste of the extended line. There would be no station here and passengers would not be allowed to alight. The inevitable problems arose – an upwardly mobile badger and a public footpath! The badger was oblivious to all the steps taken to protect its home and simply dug a new hole to its sett every time a two-way gate was placed over the last hole, to the exasperation of constructors and badger protectionists alike. The public footpath had to be fenced off from the main construction work to allow it to be used in safety – this meant that an extra line of temporary plastic fencing had to be erected. But, in spite of all these problems, the work continued apace with plans to finish the trackbed formation by Christmas 2003, followed by ballasting and track laying in 2004.

Meanwhile the company still had a tourist service to run. *Russell* had come to the end of its ten-year ticket and was laid up for a major overhaul. *Gelert* had been under repair for 3½ years and finally re-entered service on 1 August 2003 to work out the summer season. The carriage and wagon department had been revitalised and was putting in a sterling amount of work to maintain and repair the existing fleet; it also has well-researched plans to rebuild the line's

In 1963, at the Beddgelert station site, the base of the original station is prominent in the left foreground – the corrugated iron structure had been sold in the 1950s to the local policeman for £35! – while lurking in the cutting leading to the short 'Goat Tunnel' is the company's Morris Commercial 30cwt lorry. Railway construction materials are being accumulated on the right, awaiting the day when manpower might arrive to lay them. *Nick Booker collection*

Some time later the manpower has visited and the cutting, running behind The Goat Hotel, has been reclaimed by steel – a rudimentary arrangement, admittedly, but immensely significant to the participants at this juncture. *John Keylock collection*

original Buffet Car, the remains of which are in the company's ownership. The loco department, too, was seeking fresh fields to conquer, in this case the splendidly ambitious project to rebuild the Hunslet quarry loco *Lady Madcap*. This demanding project is being undertaken and financed by two members of the company's engineering department. New frames have been purchased and machined and the sheds at Llanberis have yielded many hidden treasures from the original. The project will take some time to complete, but it is one that deserves to succeed.

The railway's base at Gelert's Farm boasts a fine array of narrow-gauge diesel locomotives, matched by an equally ardent band of diesel enthusiasts. The company is home to more of these animals than on any of the other Welsh narrow-gauge lines. They range from three massive Romanian-built Lyd 2s imported from Poland, to diminutive Hunslets and Barclays, and include two recently purchased 1994-built machines. These two locos were part of a batch of six purchased from Hunslet by Balfour Beatty for use on the London Underground Jubilee Line Extension. Historically significant, they are the last locomotives of any kind to be built by the famous Leeds company. Diesels, while not strictly in keeping with Welsh Highland history, nevertheless provide an interesting genre. However, internal combustion engines are not new to the Welsh Highland – the enthusiast can point to the ground-breaking 1928 trials at Dinas of the revolutionary Kerr Stuart diesel, and even to the 1916 workings of the Dick Kerr petrol-electric machine.

The WHR(P) had become the heritage conscience of the Welsh Highland Railway, and while the South African Garratts and some distinctly non-Welsh Highland stock was operating in the north, the former '64 Company had set its sights firmly on exploiting the heritage niche. It has adopted a policy of gradually reorganising its operation in order to resemble as near as possible the railway as it had run in the 1920s. As part of this policy it was decided to recreate a typical Welsh Highland station building at Pen y Mount. The prototype was the station at Nantmor, formerly a small halt serving that isolated community and located just before the long tunnel, which led to the glories of the Aberglaslyn Pass. In 1923 environmentalist sensitivities had not yet become fashionable – the building material of the time was then the ubiquitous corrugated iron. Cheap, serviceable and readily available, it met all the essential criteria of Col Stephens. Characteristic stations were erected at Beddgelert, Nantmor and Ynysfor, while other, even lesser halts had to make do with redundant FR rolling-stock, which included covered vans and old coaches. Photographs were studied and drawings produced, the wooden framework was erected and covered with a skin of corrugated iron. The finished building boasts an open-fronted waiting shelter, combined with an office, which includes a ticket window. It certainly makes a fine addition to the Welsh Highland heritage scene.

Not content with the challenge of reconstructing a railway line, the company was to be offered yet another test of its abilities. It is well known that the renowned Col Stephens, then General Manager of the company, and one who always had an eye for a bargain, purchased in 1923 a First World War Baldwin locomotive to supplement the line's ageing motive power. Never easy to drive and distinctly unpopular, it was nicknamed 'The Goat' by its crews, but was more widely known by its War Department number of '590'. WHR(P), having devoted itself to historical accuracy, was to jump at the chance to replicate this distinctive machine when a Baldwin was offered to it by the Imperial War Museum at Duxford. As these words are typed the loan agreement is awaiting signature. It is to be hoped that this Baldwin will prove to be more popular with the staff then the original! '590' was cut up on site at Dinas after closure in 1937, but who could believe that its ghost would reappear in 2004, for it is as '590' that it will be restored to traffic by the enterprising '64 Company Limited.

So the future looks bright for the 40-year-old company whose extraordinary and often unnoticed efforts have been rewarded by the rebirth of the railway. Its optimistic, dedicated and enthusiastic approach will soon see it operating *Russell*-hauled Welsh Highland heritage trains to Pont Croesor and later to Beddgelert. And who knows, one day *Russell* may yet find itself under the dominating walls of the castle at Caernarfon, as the original proprietors of the line had always intended!

The station, shop and main entrance to the Gelert's Farm base of what is now the Welsh Highland Railway (Porthmadog) Ltd is hard by the ex-BR station in the town of Porthmadog, with the Cambrian Coast line running alongside for a short stretch, as already seen on page 72. In this view on 4 June 1977, a briefcase-toting visitor watches as a BR DMU passes the entrance, which has a token stretch of track and a wagon to entice and welcome the visitor. Note the scrub, however, to the left of the track, now the car park. *Roger Kidner*

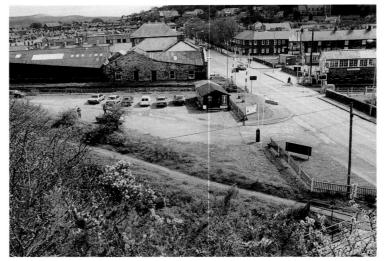

By the time of this overall view, the site has been tidied, the car-park provided and an early shop/booking office installed by the main gate. Note the level crossing on the Cambrian line, controlled by colour lights from the substantial signal box. Note, also, the course of the Gorseddau Tramway running diagonally across the lower third of the picture.

In the second view from the town's War Memorial, dated 15 September 2003, the view has again altered. The car-park is expanded, the roadside signage has been redesigned and extended, and the ex-tramway formation has been subsumed beneath tarmac. The lights controlling the crossing are still there, but now controlled by the train driver rather than the signalman, with the fine brick signal box having been demolished. At the time of this photograph, the Cambrian route had been chosen as one to test ETRMS, the latest European signalling system. *David Allan/MJS*

As is well known, volunteers are the lifeblood of any railway preservation/restoration movement. Without them, the officials of any such organisation could not function successfully, not least from an economic aspect. Early work by such 'heroes' is being undertaken at Gelert's Farm station site in 1977, with a rudimentary platform and first length of track in place. The Cambrian line is to the right.

By the time this photographer of the second view visited on 19 September 1979, much progress had been made, with track properly laid and ballasted – although still in need of a more substantial buffer stop! – but the platform surface and the distant track layout still need further attention.

The third view is undated, but quite obviously from a later period, as the station building is up and running – housing an excellent bookshop – the track is obviously in regular use and the platform is safe for all to use. *G. Jenkins/Roger Kidner/John Keylock collection*

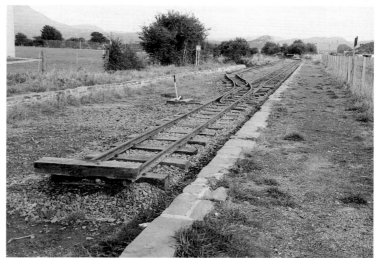

One aim of any organisation with a heritage factor is to attempt re-creation of the past. In railway terms, this includes past designs of locomotives, signalling, coaches and even station architecture. The latter aspect is superbly re-created and captured in this low-level view, using the photographer's 'eye' to excellent effect. Looking for all the world like the early years of the 20th century, it is in fact a hundred years later, 20 September 2001! The railway is to be congratulated, as is the photographer, for giving us this wonderful image. *David Allan*

The surroundings, not least the jumble of allotments, from this more elevated vantage point betray the period, but on the ground the railway is again proving itself adept at credible and convincing re-creation. On 26 October 2001 *Russell* arrives at Porthmadog terminus after a trip out and back to Pen-y-Mount. The low sun looks to be causing some problems for the engine's crew. *David Allan*

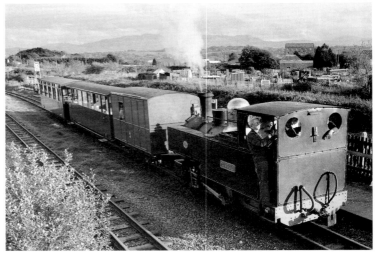

The way ahead on 5 June 1977, as the twin tracks merge into one on leaving the works complex and head out towards the sharp peak of Cnicht in the distance. Note the jumble of wagons and materials waiting their turn for attention/restoration – a sight so prevalent on heritage railways, as the organisations and sites develop. *Roger Kidner*

A dozen years have passed since the previous picture, and much has changed and appeared, not least the workshops at Gelert's Farm, seen on the left. On 13 August 1989 *Russell*, now back in near-original condition, makes a fine sight restarting the train from the brief stop at Gelert's Farm Halt, seen just beyond the last carriage. The brightly painted semaphore signal, acquired from BR, completes the picture. *Tom Heavyside*

The Engine Repair Shed here dominates the view of the Works site – though without its signboard at this time – as *Russell* is seen again, in steam, but this time receiving remedial attention from fitters. Note the typical ex-WHR water tower base on the left, here carrying the fuel oil supply. *Terry Gough*

A wider panorama of the Works site is gained in this view of 15 July 2000, showing the yard's current layout of access and sidings and with Ruston & Hornsby 1952 diesel *Glaslyn* taking pride of place. Note that the Engine Repair Shed now has a nameboard. The running line is to the extreme right of this view, with the peak and upper slopes of Moel-y-Gest beyond. *MJS*

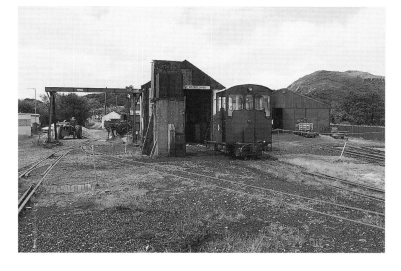

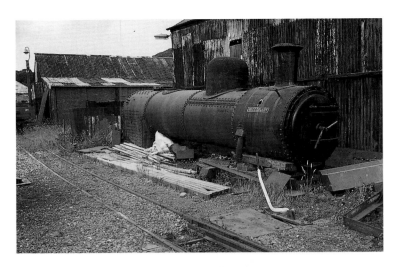

Top In the yard, also on 15 July 2000, awaiting its turn in the restoration pecking order, is ex-South African NG15 No 120 – ostensibly named *Beddgelert* – seen nestling just to the left of the Repair Shed in the previous view. Looking powerful even in this denuded form, when eventually restored to working order, together with the lengthening of the running line in conjunction with progress on restoring the WHR right into Porthmadog, this will give the WHR(P) Ltd a very useful piece of equipment. *MJS*

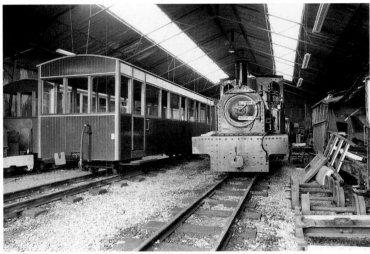

Middle While, inevitably, there is clutter in any active workshop, there is also ample evidence of the need for tidiness in the carriage shed, within the limited confines. In the first of two views inside the main Works building, *Gelert* stands next to the superb, newly constructed Eisteddfod coach, in July 1988. *Terry Gough*

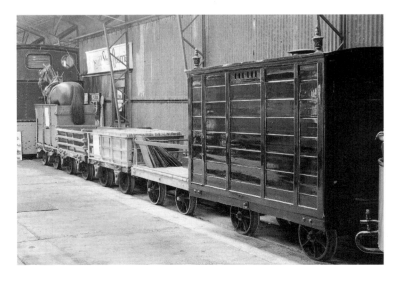

Bottom By 3 May 2002 the carriage shed is doubling as a museum, and exhibits such as the FR's famous hearse van (right), the fully laden slate wagons, and the horse dandy do much to enhance the visitor experience and encourage recommendations and revisits. *David Allan*

Above right Another item that, perhaps unknowingly, affects the visitor experience is the provision of adequate and comfortable coaching stock. Period pieces are important, but in these modern times the traveller still wants comfort – no more the 'enjoyment' of even short rides on hard, wooden, slatted seats. These factors have obviously been borne in mind in the building of No 7, seen at Gelert's Farm terminus in May 2003. There is no doubt which railway this celebrates and serves! *David Allan*

Right Also on site on the same day is No 8, the 1892 'Gladstone' coach, which has been the recipient of much labour and love in its restoration and was so-named following the visit to the railway and the use of this carriage by the Victorian Prime Minister in that year. Re-glazed, it now stands proudly with its original maroon NWNGR livery and number. *David Allan*

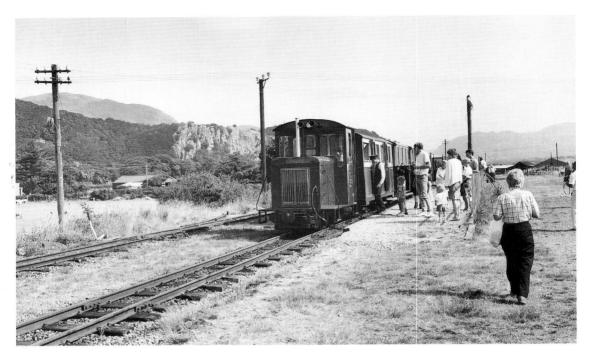

Above The other end of the line: until the railway can forge ahead north-eastwards along the old trackbed towards Pont Croesor, Pen-y-Mount is the terminus and has been since 1 August 1980. On a warm and sunny 4 August 1989, *Glaslyn*, numbered '1' in current WHR(P) stock, has run round its train and waits to transport its visitors back to Porthmadog. At this period there was no waiting shelter at this outpost. Note Tremadoc Rocks, the original sea cliffs, to the left. *MJS*

Below Recent developments at this point have seen the provision of a waiting shelter and, in true heritage fashion, it has been modelled on the original WHR corrugated iron edifice that once stood at Nantmor station, just south of the Aberglaslyn Pass. With fencing improved and signboards provided, the view in October 2002 is again towards the 'future' but, meantime, this shelter is a boon to visitors and a credit to the railway. *David Allan*

Above A glimpse of the way ahead and the prospect of exciting views of Snowdonia that it holds – not least because of the magnificent views of the mountains that will be available to future travellers – is cleverly heralded here in graphic style, with the mountains seen in the background clearly outlined on this information board for the benefit of visitors. Pen-y-Mount terminus is behind us and the tracks merely serve as a headshunt – and the limit of current operations – on 15 July 2000. *MJS*

Below Thus far and no further – at the moment. The tracks are prevented from further progress by the buffer stop and lack of permission, but the tantalising glimpse of Cnicht again on the same day reinforces future visual prospects. Eventually, the railway will steam directly towards that mountain, between the large farm building and the tall tree to its right. *MJS*

The original WHR trackbed ran alongside and to the right of the Pen-y-Mount area seen on the previous page. That formation is here seen on the extreme right, this side of the fence behind the five pairs of feet! In August 2002 serious work is continuing on installing the junction point that will eventually enable trains from Caernarfon/Beddgelert to swing into the WHR(P)'s site and its Porthmadog terminus. Planning ahead in this way is and has been essential in the successful reconstruction of the old railway. The far pointwork is an indication of current co-operation and cordial relations between the railway's constructors north and south, being provided by the 'Caernarfon end' free of charge. *David Allan*

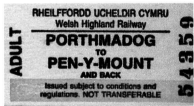

Though not entirely obvious in this view from 5 August 2001, the old trackbed forges dead ahead, immediately to the left of the large tree. Some fencing is already in situ, supplied by the railway and erected by the adjacent farmer, but until permission is granted to start work on the formation, the wooden gate (standing open here) bars the way. *David Allan*

Right At long last the green light has been given to strike out of the Beddgelert Sidings complex and make progress along the old bed, towards the immediate goal of Pont Croesor, where, hopefully, in just a few years time, there will be a grand meeting with the line coming from the north. On 3 June 2003 the lowering clouds threaten to hide Cnicht, but they cannot dampen the railway's enthusiasm and excitement at beginning work on reclaiming the trackbed. *MJS*

Below A little further on, out into the country beyond the farm building and Cynfal cottage, seen in the picture above, work is in hand on 25 April 2003, outlining the route and rolling it ready for the laying of base, track and ballast. Fencing and pegs identify the way forward. When relaid, this run will give the '64 Company's locomotives a chance to 'stretch their legs'. *David Allan*

The final stretch:
Rhyd Ddu to Porthmadog

Below left We finished our last look at Rhyd Ddu by reviewing the need for the new station site; this view clearly shows the juxtaposition of old and new. In the background, beyond the people, the old trackbed is still there as that unmade roadway, while the new railway stands on what was previously virgin field. Prince Charles visited the railway on 30 July 2003 to formally open the new extension, 'driving' the appropriately provided 1863-vintage *Prince* from Waunfawr to Rhyd Ddu. Duly honoured and adorned, the locomotive stands proudly in the new platform after the trip, while the Royal party gather at the far end of the train. The railway is now 13 miles long, the same length that the FR has enjoyed for the past 20 years. *David Allan, WHR Heritage collection*

Bottom left Meanwhile, thoughts now turn to positive consideration of progress to Beddgelert and Porthmadog. On 1 June 2003, before the celebrations just mentioned, this view, from the end of the National Park car-park, shows the original course of the railway southwards, now buried beneath rubble. The immediate stretch from here will be an extension to the headshunt of the current line, seen on the extreme left. Thereafter, within a couple of hundred yards, the old formation will be regained and will again run parallel to the road on the right. *MJS*

Above right South from Rhyd Ddu, the road runs alongside the railway trackbed until the latter swings right and passes underneath the road at Pitt's Head, so named after the image of William Pitt the Younger, twice Prime Minister between 1783 and 1806, seen in a large boulder by the side of the road at the summit of the line (650 feet). The profile seen here, from the north on a cloudy 2 June 2003, echoes one seen in a well-known cartoon of the day. Some have said it is the result of a vivid imagination! *MJS*

Below The rock at Pitt's Head is just out of the picture to the left. Here the road bridge and the trackbed beneath are heavily overgrown, demonstrating the potential flooding problems, with damp-loving plants flourishing on 24 July 1965. In 2003 this view is virtually impossible to replicate due to rampant growth, and the area will be yet another test for the new railway. *Michael Bishop*

This page Midway between Pitt's Head and Beddgelert Forest, the railway again approaches the road, then swings away on a sharp curve. In 1920, in Portmadoc, Beddgelert & South Snowdon Railway days, the track is still extant but now derelict; looking north, the road arcs towards the railway on the right. For the WHR period, onwards from 1922, this whole stretch was restored to working condition.

The railway is apparently nowhere in sight in this comparative view on 3 June 2003, but the roadway is abundantly clear, with a metal gate in the break in the wall seen above. It is hard to believe, looking at this view, that the railway could be here within a few years, especially bearing in mind the condition of the trackbed behind the photographer. *C. R. Clinker, Peter Treloar collection/MJS*

Opposite page Through Beddgelert Forest, the railway enters a cutting before threading through more tree lines to reach Beddgelert itself. Viewed from the south, this cutting is about to swallow the cut-down *Russell*, heading north towards Rhyd Ddu and, ultimately, Dinas on 8 August 1935. Seen towards the end of the line's life, the potential for nature to reclaim the area is readily apparent.

Incredibly, this is the same vantage point, as seen on 3 June 2003! Completely disguised by intervening years' growth, the cutting is still there, but now home to the line of rampant trees in the centre distance – more evidence of just what the 'restorationists' will have to face. *H. F. Wheeller, Roger Carpenter collection/ MJS*

Above North of Beddgelert there are two curved alignments. The original one was established by the erstwhile PB&SSR during the first years of the 20th century. With the coming of the WHR in 1922, this was abandoned in favour of a more tortuous route, designed to substantially ease the ruling gradient. Here we see *Russell* on a northbound train in 1923, on the later 'horseshoe' embankment. *Peter Johnson collection*

Middle and bottom Slightly closer to the station, the two trackbeds draw closer together, the left-hand one on the embankment being the WHR route, while the earlier PB&SSR line hugs the nearer shallow cutting. Note the bridge abutment still standing when photographed in 1947 and the clear view across to the distant fields.

There is no clear view on 3 June 2003! The two formations are still as above, complete with bridge abutments, but work to restore rails to the higher ground will provide some problems. *LGRP, Peter Treloar collection/MJS*

Right We are now out of the woods and on the final approach to Beddgelert station on 3 June 2003. The verdant growth evidences the damp nature of the area, and this will be a factor when replacing grass by rails. *MJS*

Above and right Turning round, the approach to the station is clear. This is 1947, ten years after trains last ran here and six years after the steel has been reclaimed – grass growth and sheep grazing have eradicated even the effects of the sleepers. Left to right in this view looking south are the station building, a water tower base and a store shed.

In 2003 only the water tower base remains, but this gives instant proof of being the same location. In this view there are no trees to remove from the proposed trackbed, but another problem will tons of animal manure! *LGRP, Peter Treloar collection/MJS*

The water tower is here in its stark glory and the station building is still in full operation, in this view in the mid-1930s. *Russell* is again the motive power, waiting for the run uphill to Rhyd Ddu, while the fireman peers from the cab, courtesy of that cut-out, after watering, and a gentleman with a bike chats to the guard by the second coach. The point lever in the foreground controls a siding to the goods shed. Driver William Hugh Williams, extreme right, watches as a visitor examines his charge.

The same view some 40 years later, on 23 May 1970, shows how nature has softened the surroundings after the disappearance of railway operations. The wagons, sleepers, etc, brought here by the '64 Company, still remain in situ.

The deposits of manure are graphically depicted here, in the comparative view of 3 June 2003. Hopefully the new railway will be a mite cleaner than this! *Lens of Sutton/John Edgington/MJS*

Right A rare sight: a photograph of *Princess* in action. 'Sister' to *Prince* already seen, she, like her 'brother', was built in 1863 for the new locomotive-hauled services over the FR, but post-1923 they both also worked over the full length of the WHR, together with their other 'brothers' *Palmerston* and *Welsh Pony*. On 31 August 1926 *Princess* pauses while *Russell* starts out from the station, returning north, the fireman again leaning out of his cab. *Princess* will then haul a service back to Portmadoc. *H. C. Casserley*

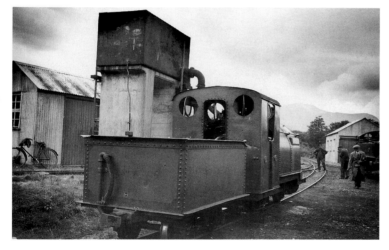

Middle and bottom This time it is *Welsh Pony*'s turn to grab the limelight, taking water at Beddgelert; *Russell* rests outside the goods shed, the crew enjoying a cigarette, while the guard, Daffyd Lloyd Hughes – seen previously – walks back towards the station.

Once more the pile of animal waste literally swamps the foreground. It will be a much more pleasant vista when locomotives return to the scene! *Millbrook House collection/MJS*

A well-known view, but a delightful and very pleasing one nevertheless: in 1924 the station is in the full flush of operations and one hopes that the four coaches were fully justified. One of the England locomotives lets off steam by the water tower, while the mixed rake of FR carriages waits for its complement of passengers. Note the view across the valley and the bookshop – closed in this view – on the right. One cannot imagine a huge number of sales from here!

The background hills and the nearside wall are constant, but elsewhere there has been great change, not least in the available view. While the trees do block out the station site and the view across the valley on 3 June 2003, they hopefully should not encroach on the running line. *Francis Frith, Peter Treloar collection/MJS*

Above **Russell** runs round its train on 9 July 1936, having brought it in from Dinas some time earlier. The three bystanders look more like enthusiasts than normal passengers, and scarcity of travellers, partly due to the poor timetabling and partly to increasing road competition, was the main cause of the cessation of operations later in the year. *S. W. Baker, WHR collection*

Below Only two years earlier, on 11 August 1934, the whole ambience of the scene is different. No doubt the railway and its staff hoped that things would continue, against all odds, but ample time to enjoy their cigarettes betrays an amount of slack in the timetable that was probably self-destructive. The ever-faithful servant *Russell* patiently waits for its next departure. *John Keylock collection*

Above This is the view southwards, with the village of Beddgelert to the left and a short coal spur in the central distance, behind the guard. Though undated, the presence of Miriam Jones (née Roberts) – garbed in traditional Welsh costume, standing under the nameboard in the station entrance – and Station Master Mr Marks points to 1934. The multi-coloured coaches proudly boast their parentage, but this will not help them in the long run. *Peter Treloar collection*

Middle and bottom Walking past the station building and turning to look back north, this was the view in 1963, with the building gone and a '64 Company wagon on site. Note the steepening slope on the right down to the village.

Forty years on all is virtually the same, with the exception of all that animal deposit! It will be interesting to see precisely where any new station building will be erected and whether the future holds an island platform, as at Waunfawr, rather than the old layout. *Nick Booker/MJS*

In this last look back at the station site, in the early 1930s, *Russell* has just arrived with a train from the north right, while on the left No 590 waits to restart its journey to Portmadoc. A schoolboy stands on the running board of the Pickering coach, admiring the sight of the ancient NWNGR locomotive. Little does he realise that it will still be around 70 years later! The crew of No 590 seem totally oblivious to the train on the other track!

We have already seen the course of the trackbed through the cutting, on the southern exit from the station site, passing behind The Goat Hotel. This is that same vantage point on 3 June 2003, just dozing before being interrupted by JCBs, etc, in a few short years, to restore the journey southwards. *J. Hughill/MJS*

Above An intriguing photograph of the carving out of a path for the railway: in the first years of the 20th century the cutting behind The Goat sees a party – no doubt made up of railway bosses, contractors and even landowners – assembled to review construction progress. It provides a fascinating insight into the work that went into creating some of the WHR – with much more primitive equipment than is available today – a fact that we all now take for granted. *Studio Eryri, WHR collection*

Below At the same period as the view above, this is the scene at the other, southern, end of the 'Goat Tunnel'. Again, the primitive constructional equipment – manpower! – is once more to the fore, as a quartet of navvies 'put shoulders to the wheel' to bring freshly hewn rock out from the tunnel, to be dumped away from the workface. Much of the spoil from this site was utilised in the construction by the PB&SSR of the aborted embankment and road bridge seen on page 100. Access to the latter would have been by the line exiting the picture bottom right, but as these rails are not set for the running line here, the rock was presumably dumped somewhere behind the photographer. *Studio Eryri/WHR collection*

Though not well known nor readily appreciated by many on and around the railway, Charles Ernest Spooner – engineer of the WHR – is buried in Beddgelert churchyard. Over the years the grave had become neglected, and a hardy group from among the railway's supporters, partly inspired and led by John Keylock, vowed to improve matters. On 17 January 1998 John is seen, centre, heavily involved in removing small trees and other detritus that had accumulated on the site, black sacks at the ready.

A mere 24 hours later the transformation is astounding. Washed clean and shiny by heavy rain, the twin gravestones of Spooner and his wife look as good as new – a real tribute to the small coteries of dedicated enthusiasts. *Both David Allan, WHR Heritage collection*

Travelling south from Beddgelert by road, one passes under what appears to be a railway bridge. Indeed, this was to have been its function, when constructed by the PB&SSR in 1905, but the original plans were abandoned and so was the bridge, now standing isolated from any practical function, like some folly. This view from the very early days of the 20th century shows workmen above and below, pausing only briefly from their labours for their portrait, wooden scaffolding still in place and a few layers of stones yet to be put in place on the bridge parapet.

As seen on 12 May 2001, fate has been kind to the bridge and its surroundings, though they have lost their 'country' feel, with height warning sign and road markings of the 20th century marring the effect. Bearing in mind the increase in traffic in the intervening years and the narrowness of passage under the bridge, it is a wonder that there have not been major collisions. How many of the thousands that pass this way annually realise the nature of the structure? *Studio Eryri/David Allan, WHR Heritage collection*

This view from the other, southern, side shows the curved nature of the approach to the bridge from this direction – again, it is surprising that no motorised demolition has occurred. The photographer has captured his friend's car as a nice period piece in this portrait of the bridge in the late evening light of 26 June 1956, still without road markings.

A slightly straighter view shows that the bridge is at an angle to the road, and this must have led to some careful consideration during construction. The date is 31 July 1969, and the presence of the Mini and the central white lines bring this view a little more up-to-date. *H. C. Casserley/John Edgington*

Left **After leaving Beddgelert the main focus of the route is the run under the road and into the Aberglaslyn Pass, for many years a favourite route for walkers. On 3 June 2003 work has begun on preparing the trackbed, both in conjunction with the provision of a new river bridge (see below) and to be ready for the eventual return of rails. With cars above and below, the levelling and consolidation of the bed is apparent, essentially relating to the new footbridge but useful for the time when rails again approach this area.** *MJS*

Above and below **The same road overbridge can just be seen darkly in the right background, partly shrouded in trees, in this view from across the water, showing the old railway's Bryn-y-Felin bridge in all its metallic glory on 22**

August 1961. Rails have long disappeared, leaving a gentle gradient to be enjoyed by thousands of walkers over the years.

Due to the deteriorating condition of the original bridge, access was initially restricted, even for walkers, followed by demolition when it was found to be beyond repair. To allay walkers' outcries, the FR assisted with provision of a new footbridge, and this is seen, from the west bank, on 3 June 2003, with the old bridge abutments on the right. The railway will eventually cross the river on the original alignment but with yet another new bridge. *Sydney Leleux/MJS*

Another view of the old bridge, date unknown but on a dull winter's day, with the trackbed leading to the Pass sweeping in from the left.

In the present view the new footbridge is in place but at a higher level than the old trackbed. At this point walkers can still enjoy the flat, level surface of the old railway, but further on into the Pass, in preparation for the railway reappearing, the public are now diverted to a fresh walkway down by the riverside. *John Keylock collection/MJS*

Opposite page The trackbed mentioned on the previous page here courses ahead towards the three tunnels in the Pass, on 5 October 1951, showing how easy the walking can be and why the area has been so popular with walkers over many years. Despite being shown on some Ordnance Survey maps as such, the alignment has never been legally open to the public as a footpath, as the railway never actually closed, being handed over, instead, to the Official Receiver. Thus the FR has been able to acquire the rights to it and to the restoration of a railway. While some decry the loss of a footpath, others savour the prospect of the Garratts steaming through these tunnels at the head of fully laden coaches to and from Porthmadog.

Seen from a similar vantage point are some of those walkers, enjoying both easy terrain and the breathtaking scenery, with magnificent hillsides above and water below, on a warm and sunny 4 August 1989. Both of these views show that future walkers will not be wholly divorced from sight of the path and, indeed, will have the added bonus of the trains returning. *Hugh Ballantyne/MJS*

Top right This fascinating view of one of the tunnels is said to date from 1922. Therefore just into WHR days, a gentleman rests with his feet apparently on some form of piping, with the floor of the trackbed a mess of stones and grass. As the railway came this way in 1923, maybe he was one of the railway's surveyors – or maybe the quoted date is incorrect. *Peter Treloar collection*

Above right In this more traditional view of the tunnels, the telegraph-wire support is still visible in the tunnel roof. This is a view looking south on 8 August 1935, when the line was still in use. *H. F. Wheeller, Roger Carpenter collection*

Right Another view from 4 August 1989, showing a party of walkers enjoying both sunshine and views. The roof of this tunnel also has metal from the railway days, but new in this shot is the provision of a gun emplacement base in the centre of the trackbed – a priority for removal, so as not to cause difficulties for the Garratts! *MJS*

A lineside view, from across the Glaslyn River, of *Welsh Pony* heading north, bound for Beddgelert from Portmadoc. With the England locomotive and the coaches once more displaying their coats of many colours, we are in FR days and the date is summer 1934. The turbulence of the water suggests recent rainfall.

Though not from exactly the same spot, this image on 12 October 2001 graphically displays the potential for both stunning photographs of the trains when they do reappear and for sheer enjoyment of those trains, the water and its surroundings. It also shows the area of the Fisherman's Path, at the lower riverside level, which walkers must now adopt following the enforced closure of the old route. *G. Simmons, Welsh Highland Heritage collection/MJS*

In another view from the PB&SSR construction period we see the southern end of the massif, and workers creating Nantmor cutting. Three levels are in use, with hand tools the order of the day – in view of the primitive tools available, it is a wonder that they created such a superb alignment and one that has stood the test of time without rock fall or blockage.

In the second photograph, from 1923, one can see just how much rock was removed, as the outcrop on which the upper-level man was standing, above, has totally disappeared, despite the line curving to the left to avoid the worst of the rock face. Once the rails were in place, how many even considered how the formation was created, I wonder?

Showing just how much nature can soften and disguise 'natural' features, this is the very same cutting as seen in July 1988, 50 years after trains last raised the echoes. It is also a credit to the determination of natural forces that trees as well as ferns and grasses can find purchase on rock.

Studio Eryri/Rail Archive Stephenson, MJS collection/Terry Gough

Nantmor station was only a couple of hundred yards south of the cutting, yet 'high and dry' and in open countryside. Note the original corrugated iron structure, now copied at Pen-y-Mount, and the old goods shed, standing clear of the 'main line'. As seen in 1939, grass and undergrowth are beginning to attack in force and soften the once clean edges of the railway. The road over the unguarded level crossing leads to the village of Nantmor.

Yes, this is the same view on 3 June 2003! No open view now, just the same open 'level crossing' and a building roughly on the site of the old station. It will be interesting to compare this view to that available after the re-arrival of the railway! *John Keylock collection/MJS*

Heading south from Nantmor, the railway crosses the road to Llanfrothen. This view from 29 August 1973 shows the blind nature of the bend from this direction, and it is to be hoped that increasing car use does not lead to problems after the new railway has arrived.

From ground level the bridge appears complete, but as can be seen from the second view by the same photographer – 12 years earlier! – this is certainly not the case at trackbed level. On 22 August 1961 two visitors – the photographer's father and brother Robin – ponder the advisability of a crossing.

By July 1988 some 'health and safety' attention has been given to the bridge, as there is now a gate protecting one end and the grass growing in 1961 has been cleared. The structure here looks in good shape and hopefully will not create too many problems for the restorationists, other than clearance of saplings, etc. *Sydney Leleux (2)/Terry Gough*

Above After crossing the road bridge, the railway gently runs down on to the plain to the south. Looking back towards Nantmor, this is the view of that graded embankment in July 1988, 50 years after the passing of the railway, now only home to sheep and wildlife. *Terry Gough*

Below Out on the plain, back in the mid-1930s, Baldwin No 590 is seen from the front carriage as it heads north, thought by your author to be pausing at Hafod-y-Llyn Halt on an unidentified service, with the hills around Nantmor and Aberglaslyn ahead of it. *H. B. Tours, MJS collection*

Above Further to the south, after leaving the heights and delights of Aberglaslyn and Nantmor, the railway is now down on flat, reclaimed land, with no road access, and eventually reaches this 'bridge to nowhere'. Crossing the Afon Dylif, situated near Croesor Junction on the old railway and roughly midway between the hamlets of Ynysfor and Garregelldrem, it should not prove any major obstacle for the renewed railway in due course. The flat nature of the surrounding land is well seen in this view from 17 January 1998. *David Allan, WHR Heritage collection*

Below Next on the original railway was Croesor Junction, where the alignment joined forces with the already existing Croesor Tramway. Due to the elaborate loop and pointwork at the junction, a station was not provided there, but a little further south, at Ynysfor, a tiny halt was provided in the middle of nowhere to serve Ynysfor Hall. *Moel Tryfan* here passes the junction loop as it heads the 1410 Portmadoc-Dinas service on 3 April 1926. *Ken Nunn Collection, MJS collection*

Pont Croesor has been mentioned earlier and here it is, seen in the 1950s. The shallow tidal waters of Afon Glaslyn stretch widely here, necessitating this wide bridge, carrying both road and rail on substantial stone pillars. In this view, with the sharp point of Cnicht once more seen in the distance, it can be seen how the railway was precariously perched on the near side on steel beams resting on the piers, with no safety parapet!

Fifty years later and the road bridge remains, as do the stone pillars, but all evidence of a railway has disappeared and the vantage point is becoming blocked by tree growth.

Yet more tree growth precludes access to the 'past' vantage points, but this is the view on 3 June 2003, with little change other than the foliage. *John Keylock collection/ Terry Gough/MJS*

Right This is the view looking the other way on 3 June 2003, towards Porthmadog, with the car parked on the old trackbed. There is potential difficulty here due to the road swinging through 90 degrees, immediately after the end of the bridge. Careful consideration will have to be given to a suitable level crossing design to meet current Health & Safety standards. *MJS*

Below Further along the trackbed towards Porthmadog there is more evidence of what work will be needed by the volunteers of WHR(P) as they strive to carve their way to this point from Gelert's Farm. One hopes that the underlying foundation is still sound. *David Allan, WHR Heritage collection*

Above We have now reached 'civilisation' and the outskirts of Portmadoc/Porthmadog. With the future site of Gelert's Farm and the WHR(P) to the right of this view, No 590 stands at the second Portmadoc (New) station in 1934, with a train bound for Beddgelert. The driver discusses some matter with a member of the public, while the guard prepares to join the train and a lady approaches from Portmadoc. The reason for a second (New) station was the crossing of the Cambrian line on the level, situated immediately behind this train. Prior to 1929, the original station lay the other (Portmadoc) side of the crossing, but post this date, passengers had to detrain here and walk across the standard gauge to reach Portmadoc – certainly not conducive to encouraging increased patronage! It will be interesting to see how the new WHR fares in crossing the current Cambrian line. *J. Hughill*

Opposite top Looking in the opposite direction, a work-weary *Russell* has drawn to a stand at the new station in 1934, with a train from Dinas. The grinning lady, carrying baskets and coat, is giving support to the poor soul attempting to alight, betraying the rudimentary (or complete lack of) facilities at this latter-day terminus. Two children wait for the exercise to finish. To the left of the locomotive, the driver approaches a customer. Note the stone weigh house in the right background. *Real photographs, Peter Treloar collection*

Middle and bottom On the 'other side of the tracks' is the site of the original 1923 Portmadoc (New) station, no longer a through facility but with the nameboard still in position in this view of the early 1930s. The water tower on the left, without its tank, and the grass beginning to sprout between the rails evidence the change in fortunes. The signal box that formerly controlled the flat crossing of the Cambrian line can be seen in the left distance, while to the right of it is the white building of the new 1929 (New) station. The Prenteg outcrop dominates the distant horizon.

With the fencing and overgrown nature of the site today, it is difficult to visualise the railway ever having run here – certainly with enough room for two tracks! This was the view on 3 June 2003, with the water tower base still defying all logic and remaining in situ. *John Keylock collection/MJS*

Looking north from the points giving access to the Flour Mill Loop, on the final approaches to the town of Portmadoc in 1948, 11 years after cessation of traffic on the WHR, rails are still in place between the substantial bridge parapet as they cross Y Cyt drainage channel. With the cliffs behind Tremadoc in the distance, the railway could almost still be imagined to be in service. The building to the left of the tracks was the old station building, which stood at a lower level than the trackbed and survived until the late 1990s. The black building is on the far side of the Cambrian line.

The site on 3 June 2003 was more jungle than railway, as the use of this stretch has diminished greatly during recent years, since the course of the footpath has been re-routed. The new railway will have fun negotiating this area! *LGRP, Peter Treloar collection/MJS*

Here is a sight to delight enthusiasts and historians alike, but the thought of the railway once again running through the streets of Porthmadog fills many local inhabitants with fear and loathing. While this is the final aim of the new railway, to reclaim the access to and junction with the FR at Harbour station, this particular route will not be similarly reclaimed. This view from 1925, however, gives a taste of what was, as *Prince* runs the final 100 yards or so into the FR's station. Note how the leading three (FR) coaches seem in grave danger of grounding on the road!

It goes without saying that road traffic has mushroomed since the 1920s, not least in the holiday town of Porthmadog. Indeed, such are the current volumes in summer months that I was not able to stand in the earlier photographer's precise footsteps, for fear of my life! Teetering off the edge of the curb, however, this is a contemporary view, on 3 June 2003. *H. G. W. Household/MJS*

When the new railway finally reaches Harbour station, this will again be the entrance for the WHR to FR territory, and once more the residents of Britannia Terrace will have the delights of steam trains running past their front doors. In 1925 *Moel Tryfan* opens up for the long run north to Dinas, with the ubiquitous sand bucket securely lodged by the smokebox door and one of the Ashbury coaches in tow.

The current comparative view of 3 June 2003 shows the proximity of the road to the old trackbed and how relatively easy will be the reinstatement of the old track route, assuming due cognisance is taken of potentially conflicting road traffic movements! *Photomatic, Peter Treloar collection/MJS*

Another view of the final link: with the FR's tracks behind and to the right of this train, the WHR's coaches stand on the spur behind *Welsh Pony*, waiting to depart with a train of two Ashburys and a Pickering for the very short trip to the 1923 Portmadoc (New) station in 1934.

The way may look blocked by the FR's landscaping, in this view from 3 June 2003, but again it will be a relatively simple job to re-lay tracks on the line of the old spur and finally give travellers the ability, should they so wish, of travelling nearly 40 miles – from Dinas to Blaenau Ffestiniog – through truly magnificent scenery behind some of the best narrow-gauge locomotives in the world. *Real Photographs, Peter Treloar collection/MJS*

Our final look at Porthmadog is a superb aerial portrait of the modern west end of the Cob (lower centre). Harbour station (left centre) and Britannia Bridge (upper centre). Rather than retracing the steps of the old railway through the streets, however, the new proposal is for the line to shadow the far bank of the river (upper right corner), before swinging onto and across the bridge and finally slewing into Harbour station. With just this short stretch to interrupt road traffic, there is widespread and official support for the project and it holds out a mouth-watering prospect before (hopefully) the end of this decade. *David Allan collection*

PORTRAITS

Top Understandably – and deservedly – *Russell* holds a very special place in the hearts and minds of aficionados of the original WHR and its heritage future. Built by Hunslet of Leeds (as Works No 901) in 1906, the 2-6-2T is seen here still in 'as built' condition, at Beddgelert in October 1923, with driver William Hugh Williams standing guard over his charge. *LGRP, Peter Treloar collection*

Middle After operations on the WHR effectively came under the same management as the FR – and not long after the above view – *Russell* was 'cut down' to accommodate the more restricted loading gauge of the FR and to allow the possibility of the locomotive running over that railway's metals. This new status is seen on the other track at Beddgelert on 8 August 1935. Note how the air pump has disappeared and the chimney, dome and cab have all been reduced in height. The roof required a half-moon to be bitten from it to accommodate the height of the engine's crew! Note the jacket nonchalantly draped over the back of the cab – this also happened during journeys and one wonders if any were lost en route! *H. F. Wheeller, Roger Carpenter collection*

Bottom When the railway gave up the ghost in 1937, *Russell* was initially abandoned in the shed at Dinas, but was rescued from there to spend many years wandering around industrial railways (see Volume 1 for details). Finally, a return to the Principality was arranged and *Russell* returned home on 24 August 1955. This is the view of its arrival at Tywyn, on the Talyllyn Railway, where time was then spent on display in the open air. *David Rouse, Welsh Highland collection*

Top In 1962 *Russell* was at Carnforth, where repairs and remedial work were undertaken. This view, inside the shed, appears to show a new, higher-edged cab roof, but this is merely an optical illusion, created by the close proximity of the tank locomotive immediately beyond. *A. R. Taylor,* Railway Magazine *collection*

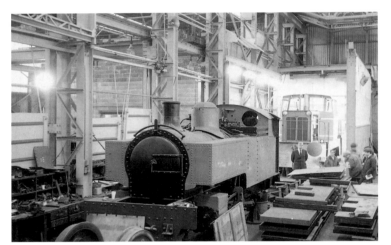

Middle By 1970 another move had been made, this time to Hunslet Engineering's Works in Leeds. Seen here in much plusher conditions that those at Carnforth, on 26 March of that year, *Russell* stands in line to receive a new boiler, with Hunslet's own Sentinel diesel No 6982 behind. With a handful of young enthusiasts also present, this was obviously an organised tour. *Sydney Leleux*

Bottom Restored to working condition in July 1987 by the '64 Company, this view shows the old man 'back home' and once more restored to near original condition. Proudly on display by Caernarfon's water tower on the new WHR, this visit to the 'top end' of the line on 16 September 2000 was a distinct bonus for all concerned and a glimpse of what might have been, had the early intentions of extending the WHR from Dinas to Caernarfon come to pass. *MJS*

The first of these three examples of differing forms of motive power on the original NWNGR/WHR. is Vulcan Foundry Ltd 0-6-4T *Snowdon Ranger*, seen by the signal box and smithy at Dinas on 23 June 1909. Delivered in 1875 to the NWNGR, and receiving repairs and some rebuilding in 1902, parts of the locomotive were used in 1917, in combination with others from fellow single-Fairlie *Moel Tryfan*, to fabricate a 'new' *Moel Tryfan*, with the remaining parts despatched for scrap. *H. L. Hopwood, Ken Nunn Collection, MJS collection*

On the same date, *Gowrie* stands coupled to its train at South Snowdon, prior to returning to Dinas. Purchased by the NWNGR from Hunslet the previous year, it served the railway for just seven years, departing for the Ministry of Munitions during the First World War. An opportunity came in 1923 to reclaim the locomotive, then languishing in a Darlington scrapyard, but that option was not taken, the railway rather taking possession of an ex-WD Baldwin 4-6-0T (see below). *H. L. Hopwood, Ken Nunn Collection, MJS collection*

Baldwin No 590 is seen at the second Portmadoc (New) station, with coach No 27 in tow, around 1935. Arriving in July 1923, its size ensured its use solely on the WHR, with brief excursions into the FR's Harbour station and visits to Boston Lodge Works. It received a red coat in 1934, when the FR reputedly numbered it 13 – though there is no photographic evidence – but this life was short-lived, scrapping coming in 1942. *H. B. Tours, MJS collection*

Above From 1923 the FR sent several of its locomotives to WHR metals, including the four 1863-vintage England 0-4-0STs, to help ease shortages in motive power. Of these, perhaps the most regular visitor was *Prince*, here seen at Beddgelert, looking somewhat battle weary, in 1925. *R. J. Plummer, Welsh Highland Heritage collection*

Below Over the years *Prince* has seen many occasions, anniversaries and rebuildings. All three elements come together in this portrait of the 'mighty flea' celebrating its 140th year by being an indispensable part of the opening of the WHR extension to Rhyd Ddu and the 'Super Power Weekend' of 14 September 2003. On that day it is seen rounding Fridd Isaf curve at the head of the 1540 Caernarfon-Rhyd Ddu two-coach train – visions of 1923! *MJS*

Above Another VIP – on the FR and, in the not too distant future, on the WHR – for the last 40 years, is K1, the world's first Garratt. Completed in 1909 at Beyer Peacock's Manchester Works, K1 and 'sister' K2 were designed and built for work in Tasmania. Their working lives ended there in 1929, after which they spent 20 years in store. Their story is told in Volume 1, explaining how what is now known as K1 washed up at the FR's Harbour station in 1966, as seen here on static display on 19 July of that year. *MJS collection*

Below Just short of another four decades have passed and, at last, after many years of loving attention and devotion by committed volunteers, the locomotive is fast approaching complete restoration to running order. Inside the FR's Boston Lodge Works on 4 June 2003, renovated parts have been re-assembled and K1 is beginning to look like its old self again. *MJS*

Above For the comfort and/or enjoyment of the travelling public, the new WHR has created/re-created both old and new in coaching stock. On 1 June 2003 the brilliant and highly attractive recreation of NWNGR No 24 stands at the head of more modern stock, waiting for the locomotive to form the 1415 service to Waunfawr. Though built on original NWNGR axle-boxes, the coach is a new build, albeit to past design. The original No 24 was one of two 'summer' (semi-glazed) coaches purchased by the NWNGR in 1894 from builders Ashbury. Initially No 12, it was renumbered 24 after 1923, then to 23 in 1936. This coach still exists, as No 23 in green livery, with this new one now following consecutive numbering. *MJS*

Below For the opening of the very first stretch of the revitalised WHR, from Caernarfon to Dinas, the railway commissioned attractive and comfortable purpose-built carriages, constructed to a slighter larger loading gauge and certainly with more creature comforts than those possessed by the old company. On 12 October 1997, on the day before formal opening, No 2020, the only unglazed example, stands in pristine condition at Dinas. *MJS*

TIMETABLES

TIME TABLE FOR JULY, AUGUST, SEPTEMBER, 1892.
ALL TRAINS FIRST, SECOND AND THIRD CLASS.

Tourists should make sure of Cheap Coach Tickets for Beddgelert, by purchasing them before leaving Dinas.

FARES CARNARVON.			FARES DINAS.		
SINGLE.	RETURN.		SINGLE.	RETURN.	

CONDITIONS.—The arrival time denotes when trains may be expected. The Directors give notice that the trains shall start or arrive at the time specified in the Time Bills, nor will they be answerable for any loss, inconvenience, or injury, which may arise from delays or detention ; but attention will be paid to ensure punctuality, as far as practicable. The Published Time Bills of the Company are only intended to fix the time at which Passengers may be certain to obtain their Tickets for any journey from the various Stations.

Passengers change carriage at Dinas to and from Carnarvon by London and North Western Railway.

TRAINS DO NOT RUN ON SUNDAYS.

S. TANNER,
SECRETARY & MANAGER.

Dinas Station, near Carnarvon, June 25, 1892.
W. Smith, Printer, Llandudno.

The public timetable for the North Wales Narrow Gauge Railways for the summer of 1892 (*above*), and a working timetable for the Welsh Highland Railway effective from 9 July 1923.

Down Trains.

Distance from Portmadoc (New Station)		Station		1 Sh Engine and Slates E.X	2 Pass	3 Pass	4 Sh Eng Goods and Slates SX	5 Pass	6 Pass	7 Pass.	8 Pass. B
M.	C.			A.M.	A.M.	A.M.	P.M.	P.M.	P.M.	P.M.	P.M.
		aPortmadoc (New St.)	dpt	7 15	8 45	10 53		1 30	3 55	6 30	
1	75	Pont Croesor	,,		8A56			1A41	4A 6	6A41	
2	75	Ynysfor	,,		9A 2	11A 8		1A47	4A12	6A47	
3	25	Croesor Junct	arr	7 35			A	A	A	A	
3	77	Hafod Garregog	dpt	A			A	A	A	A	
4	77	Hafod y Llyn	,,		9 18	11 23		2 3	4 28	7 3	
5	59	Nantmor	,,		9 30	11 35		2 15	4 40	7X15	
7	77	aBeddgelert	arr		10X10	12X15		3x30	4X50		8 25
		Do	dpt		A			A	A		A
10	2	Hafod Ruffydd	,,					A	A		A
10	78	Pitts Head	,,		10 42	12 45		4 0	5 20		8 55
12	2	aSouth Snowdon	arr		10x50	1X 0		4X 5	5 25		9X 0
		Do	dpt		11 2	1 13		4 17	5 38		9 13
14	2	Quellyn Lake	,,		11 11						
		Salem	,,		A	A		A	A		A
16	62	Bettws Garmon	,,		11A14	1A26			5A51		9A26
17	42	aWaenfawr	arr		11 19	1 31		4 32	5 56		9 31
		Do	dpt		11 21	1 35		4 38	6X 0		9 35
		Bryngwyn	dpt				4 0				
19	22	aTryfan Junction	arr		11 29	1 43	4 25	4 43	6 8		9 43
		Do	dpt		11 32	1 46	4 29	4 46	6 11		9 46
21	22	aDinas	arr		11 42	1 55	4 40	4 55	6 20		9 55

Light Engines from Boston Lodge	Station		Pass.
	Boston Lodge	dpt	6 55
	Portmadoc (Old St)	arr	6 59
	Do.	dpt	7 5
	Portmadoc (New St.)	arr	7 10

Up Trains.

Distance from Dinas		Station		1 Sh Eng Goods and Slates	2 Pass	3 Pass	4 Pass	5 S. X. Sh Eng Goods and Slates	6 Pass	7 Pass	8 Pass
M.	C.			A.M.	A.M.	A.M.	NOON	P.M.	P.M.	P.M.	P.M.
		aDinas Junction	dpt		9 45	12 0	2 0	3 10	5 40	8 0
2	0	aTryfan Jct.	arr		9 54	12 9	2 15	3 19	5 49	8 9
			dpt		9 57	12 13	2 19	3 22	5 52	8 13
		Bryngwyn	arr				2 45			
3	60	aWaenfawr	arr		10 5	12 20		3 30	5 59	8 21
			dpt		10 9	12 24		3 33	6X 5	8 25
4	40	Bettws Garmon	,,		10A14	12A29		3A38	6A10	8A30
		Salem	,,		A	A		A	A	A
7	20	Quellyn Lake	,,		A	A		A	A	A
			dpt		10 31	12 46		3 55	6 29	8 49
9	20	aS. Snowdon	arr		10 40	12 55		4 2	6 39	8 59
			dpt		10X46	12X59		4X10	6 43	9X 8
10	24	Pitts Head	,,		A	A		A	A	A
11	20	Hafod Ruffydd	,,		A	A		A	A	A
13	25	aBeddgelert	arr		11 11	1 25		4 35	7 7	9 33
			dpt		9X33	11X38	2X20	4X45	7X20	
15	43	Nantmor	,,		9 45	11 50	2 32	4 57	7 32	
16	25	Hafodyllyn	,,		A	A	A	A	A	
17	20	Hafod Garregog	,,		A	A	A	A	A	
17	77	Croesor Junct	,,	7 45	A	A	A	A	A	
18	17	Ynysfor	,,		10A 1	12A 6	2A48	5A13	7A48	
19	27	Pont Croesor	,,		10A 7	12A12	2A54	5A19	7A54	
21	22	aPortmadoc (New St)	arr	8 30	10 18	12 20	3 5	5 30	8 5	

Light Engines from Boston Lodge	Station		Pass.
	Portmadoc (New St)	dpt	8 10
	Portmadoc (Old St)	arr	8 15
	,,	dpt	8 30
	Boston Lodge	arr	8 34

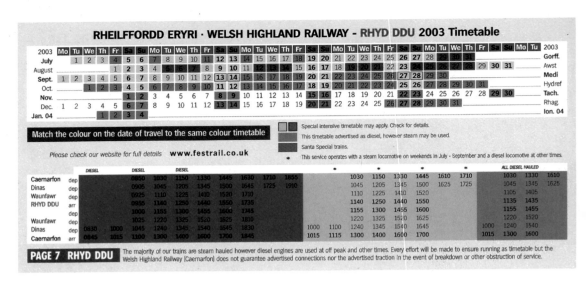

The WHR Caernarfon-Rhyd Ddu timetable for 2003.

INDEX